BOAT BUILDING *and* BOAT YARDS *of* LONG ISLAND

BOAT BUILDING *and* BOAT YARDS *of* LONG ISLAND

A Tribute to Tradition

NANCY SOLOMON

Foreword by Bill Bleyer

Published by The History Press
Charleston, SC
www.historypress.com

First published 2021

Manufactured in the United States

ISBN 9781467145213

Library of Congress Control Number 2021948329.

Notice: The information in this book is true and complete to the best of our knowledge. It is offered without guarantee on the part of the author or The History Press. The author and The History Press disclaim all liability in connection with the use of this book.

CONTENTS

FOREWORD

If it wasn't for a few dedicated historians and cultural ethnographers, including Nancy Solomon, Long Island residents might forget how important the waterways were to the exploration, development and identity of the region.

Current-day residents usually don't think much about the waterways unless they are out on them for recreation. But if it wasn't for the Atlantic Ocean, Long Island Sound and numerous bays and rivers, the island would never have been settled and developed the way that it was because travel by land was arduous.

To take advantage of these water routes, the island's inhabitants turned to local shipyards and boat builders, a handful of which remain, some still using traditional materials and skills.

These boat builders have wonderful, colorful stories—stories that would inevitably be lost if it wasn't for folklorist Nancy Solomon gathering and preserving them. It's especially important to preserve the stories of the boat builders and the history of the boat yards because these time capsules are continually threatened by development of their waterfront sites and storms like 2012's Superstorm Sandy. When they're gone, all we will have is the historical record, now thankfully augmented by Nancy's compilation.

I've had the pleasure of knowing Nancy since the late 1980s, when she began to accumulate local folklore and oral histories in Freeport. She quickly became a great source on local maritime history for my stories when I covered that subject for *Newsday*. And after moving to Long Island Traditions in 1991, she remained a good source, even after I left the paper in 2014 to freelance and write books on Long Island history, particularly for my 2019 book, *Long Island and the Sea: A Maritime History.* Nancy graciously supplied valuable information for my chapter on shipyards and boat building.

I could use only a small amount of information on the subject, so it's great that Nancy has been able to expand it into a full volume.

It's a great resource, and I hope others appreciate it as much as I do.

Bill Bleyer
Bayville, Long Island, May 2021

ACKNOWLEDGEMENTS

When I began this project in 2010, it was in response to the loss of several boat yards and working waterfront cultural resources around Long Island. Inspired by several journalists, including Bill Bleyer, I began documenting the boat builders I had come to know since the late 1980s. Several people encouraged me, including Robert MacKay, then director of Preservation Long Island; Tania Werbizky, formerly of the Preservation League of New York; and Kristin Herron of the New York State Council on the Arts, which helped support our exhibit *From Shore to Shore: Boat Builders of Long Island and Westchester*. My colleague, folklorist Tom Van Buren, formerly of Arts Westchester and co-curator of the exhibit, was my partner as we explored the traditions of boat builders and boat yards on Long Island and Westchester. His understanding of the boat building tradition was instrumental in my education. I have learned much from the people featured in this publication, and I thank them for their willingness to work with me and Long Island Traditions. Ann Latner, program director at Long Island Traditions, helped edit this manuscript, and Regina Feeney assisted in researching and writing several chapters in this book. Banks Smithers of The History Press has been very helpful and supportive during this process, and I thank him for his encouragement and patience. Finally, many thanks to all the boat builders and boat yard owners featured in this book. Your generosity overwhelms me, and I thank you.

INTRODUCTION

When I was in ninth grade, my family moved to Mamaroneck on Long Island Sound in Westchester County so that we could be closer to our sailboat. Living across the street from Nichol's Boat Yard on Rushmore Avenue, I went to the yard frequently to see who was working on their boat, a never-ending task in the spring months, and observe the lobstermen and commercial fishermen who docked their boats there. I eventually learned about the intricacies of sailboat and motorboat designs, how centerboards gave way to large keels as the boat increased in size and how different types of craft changed functions over time, reflecting the shift from commercial fishing to recreational fishing and boating. The lessons I learned from the boat yard crews have stayed with me throughout my life.

In 1987, I began working as a folklorist and architectural historian on Long Island, documenting the maritime culture and architecture of Long Island's north and south shores, in order to help educate residents and visitors about the long heritage of these traditions, in the hopes of preserving them for future generations. At first, I focused on the working fishermen and baymen, alongside recreational tradition bearers, whose way of life had undergone significant changes over the last fifty years. The LI Arts Council at Freeport, followed by Long Island Traditions, where I have worked since 1991, supported these efforts, so that we could acknowledge the vast talents and skills of those who carry on maritime traditions, including the local ecological knowledge that has shaped their way of life. Soon afterward I began learning about the tradition of boat builders on Long Island, a region that has long been recognized as a maritime center for the industry.

BOAT BUILDERS

Boat builders have a long history in our region, beginning with the modest skiffs, garveys and dories used by Long Island baymen and fishermen of European, African American and Native American background. They practice a traditional art involving the sawing, shaping, treating and fitting of wood into a boat. The skills necessary to produce a wooden boat are similar to house carpentry but distinct in the design and construction processes. Boat builders use a variety of woodcraft tools, including the steam box used to bend wood, handmade planes and chisels and saws and drills of all kinds to work with the huge variety of local and imported wood available to builders and restorers. While many of the traditional crafts have survived to the present day, the local boat building industry has declined, reflecting technological changes in water transportation and fishing in our region. The builders featured encompass different traditions, but most share one important perspective: restoration work has replaced building as their primary revenue source, due to the expense of labor-intensive wooden boat building. Those featured in this publication are a sample of traditional builders, defined as those who learned informally from master

The *Lady Diane*, built by Howard Pickerell. *Photo by Nancy Solomon, 2011.*

Davison's Boatyard, circa 1945. *Courtesy of Dan Schmidt.*

craftsmen, who pass down the traditions to the next generation. Many were still working as of this writing. It is important to understand that this is not a history book but one that examines the history of traditional boat builders and boat yards.

Boat Yards

The boat yards featured are only a small selection of the many traditional yards that have lined Long Island coasts and canals. Selected according to their long history and historic structures, they are vanishing as real estate prices escalate for their prime waterfront locations. Rising property taxes and a diminished market have tested the survival of boat yards in our region, as work in the yards shifted from production to maintenance, restoration and repair. Historic features of the boat yard landscape are also fading, as some yards have gradually replaced their marine railways with slips and travel lifts to make way for more lucrative yard uses. Other yards have also incorporated marinas into their property. "Retired" yards are also used for new commercial and residential developments, drastically changing the character of our working waterfronts. Some of the yards featured here defy these trends, retaining their historic functions and structures, while others have succumbed to the pressures facing them. Whether large or small, infamous or humble, each boat yard has played a special role in our shared history.

HISTORIC PRESERVATION

Recent storms and hurricanes, such as Superstorm Sandy, emphasize the importance of preserving these unique traditions, in the wake of damage rivaling the "Long Island Express" of 1938, Hurricane Donna in 1960 and Hurricane Irene in 2011. While some boat yards were able to avoid serious damage through their location or preemptive measures, those affected were hard hit. Severe flooding damaged buildings, docks, equipment and boats. While repair has been an arduous and costly experience, some yards have unfortunately suffered irreparable losses. In the years to come I hope to continue the documentation and preservation of these traditions and invite you to join our efforts.

—Nancy Solomon
Executive Director of Long Island Traditions

Part I

NORTH SHORE BOAT BUILDERS AND BOAT YARDS

Long Island's north shore is approximately 118 miles, consisting of numerous harbors and villages well known for their boat building history. In this section, we surveyed two historic boat yards and interviewed seven traditional boat builders, defined as those who have carried on the traditions of previous generations. Many of the boats constructed on the north shore are sailboats, due to the popularity of Long Island Sound as a center of sailboat racing and pleasure boating since the mid-nineteenth century. The Hanff Boat Yard and the Clarke Boat Yard span over 150 years, making them unofficial historic landmarks. The boat builders carry on a legacy that is equal to the yards. The builders profiled all work in wood or fiberglass, sharing traditions that have changed over time. They have also shared trade practices and insights that result in durable vessels. In the chapters that follow, you will meet and learn about this historic industry and the challenges boat yard managers and builders currently face. I encourage you to visit the yards that are accessible and talk to owners of the vessels created.

1

ANDERS LANGENDAL

Master Boat Builder and Restorer
Greenport

Greenport is a small town that swells in the summer with tourists and second home owners, transforming the quiet community into a bustling seaside resort. Behind the village's main drag is the Clarke Boat Yard, where Anders Langendal works to restore classic wooden vessels and recreational boats.

Anders Langendal was born in Sweden, just outside Stockholm, in 1944. His family lived in the suburbs of Stockholm, where his father was an architect and his mother was a nurse. Anders recalls that the family always had small boats, which he remembers from the age of three.

In 1959, at the age of fifteen, he started as an apprentice at a shipyard two hours from Stockholm. Anders recalls that "in those days it was a four-year apprenticeship. It was a continuation of high school. In Sweden, I was well known for building 5.5s, which was Olympic class in those days. It was a 30-foot sailboat—beautifully built, varnished mahogany." Anders worked at Kungsörs Boatyard, then owned by Oscar Schelin, a famous sailor and builder. Anders built a sailboat, designed in part by Schelin, at the end of his apprenticeship.

The small sloop boat was planked and had traditional *lund* seams, varnished mahogany, on oak frames. It measured over five meters. Like other apprentices, Anders built that boat and sold it at the Swedish boat show. With the earnings, he flew to New York to the National Boat Show. He was approached by Victor Oslan, a potential customer, who asked if he could build him a boat, leading Anders to the Clarke Boat Yard in Greenport.

Anders Langendal (*far left*) works with a Swedish boat crew. *Courtesy of Anders Langendal.*

"When I came here, about fifty people were working here, seven good carpenters, machinists, painters and roustabouts. In those days, there were three classes of workers, and you would start as third or second class. Within three months, I got first-class pay." By the mid-1960s, the Greenport boat yard where he worked was in decline. "The last boat built here was a fifty-four-foot yawl—launched in 1966."

Anders brought traditional skills with him such as "tight planking" and steaming wood in a steam box that is used today. "I went on my own after that. Almost every building near the water out in Greenport I have rented at one time or another. Not so much building but restoring and repairing boats."

"We cut our own wood. We sliced up the timbers to the size we wanted—mostly white oak—and then store it—stack it and let them air dry. Then we use it when we have to. People that cut trees know we always want logs. We can tell if there are not too many knots in it. We prefer that they are cut in the wintertime. It makes the grain a little tighter."

Like other builders, Langendal restores historic wooden boats, enabling him to preserve skills he learned in Sweden. He has built several skiffs and sailboats for both recreational and commercial fishermen, the most recent one completed in 2020.

The boat shed. *Photo by Nancy Solomon, 2011.*

> *I've worked on different types of fishermen boats, all wooden. It doesn't make a difference if it's a pleasure boat or commercial boat. They are basically the same except commercial boat has to be inspected by the Coast Guard. Other than that, a boat is a boat. In the last ten to fifteen years or so—there's been a lot of restoration or rebuilding of wooden boats. The easiest boats to repair are the ones that haven't been messed with. When you take an old boat apart you can see a lot of history through the years. You learn a lot from that.*

Newer technologies have helped builders because they are often lighter and easier to use. However, some tools are many years old.

> *My favorite old tool is Stanley block plane. A lot of the special tools we make ourselves. One thing that has changed is that we have lighter tools. The lightweight power tools and hand tools are easier to use these days because you can move around. Big ships, forty-two-foot ships are enormous, but the small machines can do a great job. They are not quite as good as the old ones, but things aren't so heavy anymore. It's not often that we put in a two-inch old plank in a boat anymore. If it is, we can fashion them up with power planes, hand planes.*

Langendal works on large ferry boats such as *The Commander*. *Photo by Nancy Solomon, 2011.*

Anders Langendal, 2011. *Photo by Nancy Solomon.*

Surprisingly, the process for restoration has changed little: "When I started out in the '50s, we had to hand sand our boats. Boats were like a mirror. They had a beautiful finish." When most people think of boat builders, they often assume that they only build boats from scratch. Yet many boat builders spend a great deal of time restoring boats as well. "For some of the boats, rebuilding is like building a whole new boat because there was not much left on them," recalled Anders. "In the last ten to fifteen years or so—there's been a lot of restoration or rebuilding of wooden boats."

Today, Anders's sons Christian and Eric work alongside him and have built boats of their own. "My two sons got into it because they were always hanging around the shipyard." They grew up on Shelter Island, where Anders and his family have lived since the 1960s. They expect to keep working for years to come. "We have lots of projects. I don't think I've been out of work a day in my life."

2

BAYLES BOAT SHOP

Port Jefferson

Across Long Island there are several volunteer groups that build or restore historic boats. The nonprofit Long Island Seaport and Eco Center started one such project in 1995. The Bayles Boat Shop has evolved into an ongoing program at the Port Jefferson Village Center, located adjacent to one of the original Bayles Shipyard's restored buildings, built about 1917. The shop is located on Port Jefferson Harbor on the former site of the Bayles Shipyard. The Bayles Boat Shop was built in 2006 by the Timber Framers Guild using traditional framing methods. Men and women, teenagers and retirees, gather on Wednesday and Saturday mornings, learning about and working together on power and sailing vessels, old and new. Two boat restoration/building projects take place simultaneously in the timber-framed boat shop.

The shop's projects are suggested in several ways. A boat owner may ask the group to restore their vessel, paying the group for materials and a modest fee for their time. Such projects can take several weeks or several months, depending on the condition of the vessel. The group also constructs new watercraft, which may later be sold or auctioned off, to help raise money for the nonprofit organization. Occasionally, the group restores a historic vessel that is later sold to an individual.

Their restoration projects are perhaps the most challenging. As volunteer Charles Kenny explained, "[A] restoration project generally involves many surprises. You have to understand what the builder was thinking. Why he fashioned pieces a certain way even if you have a set of drawings or

Charles Kenny teaches one of the volunteers. *Photo by Nancy Solomon, 2011.*

The Bayles Boat Shop. *Photo by Nancy Solomon, 2011.*

plans, frequently a builder will utilize different approaches which are not depicted in the plans or drawings. It is a lot of fun, detective work. But it is slow going."

Approximately twenty-seven volunteers work at the boat shop, including former carpenters, engineers, lawyers and people from different backgrounds. The boats have included a 1928 historic "SS" class sloop designed by Benjamin Hallock in about 1906. The 1928 Hallock SS boat was completed in 2013, a process that took over twelve months. Over twenty people worked on the project. Kenny noted, "This particular project was a very extensive restoration."

The volunteers come from varied walks of life. Charles Kenny explained how he got involved:

> *I grew up on the water, Great South Bay, Bay Shore, Long Island, New York. I had a fascination with boats. They were still using wooden craft in the mid-'50s. My first boat was a fifteen-foot Old Town cedar lapstrake on oak frames. It was ten years old. I maintained that vessel for five years. I did some structural repairs when the boat was damaged. As a youngster, I would build boat houses and little rafts that could launch in water.*

Charles Kenny demonstrates how to cut and install a rib to a new volunteer. *Photo by Nancy Solomon, 2011.*

Another important person at the shop is Betty Arink, once president of the Long Island Seaport Eco Center, which owns the shop. Arink has worked on several boats at the shop and is also a volunteer at the Long Island Maritime Museum's boat building shop. She comes from a long line of boat owners who have been involved in restoring and preserving historic vessels in the region.

There are several lumberyards where boat builders can find materials, including Harned's Mill in Commack and Condon Lumber in White Plains. Using original or replicas of the vessels' drawings, the men and women restore or build from scratch various types of historic wooden vessels, from modest shallow-water skiffs and contemporary kayaks to lobster boats and racing yachts. Typical tasks include replacing rotting ribs, planking and other structural components. A wide variety of saws and planers are used, some of which are more than seventy-five years old. According to Kenny,

> *You really need to bring in a number of skills, the most important one is to be able to read a set of plans. The other important skill is to measure properly and operate the tools in a way that doesn't abuse the tool and does not make the operation unsafe for use.*
>
> *Most of us grew up on the water as youngsters. Our economy and culture was driven by maritime history up until the last forty or fifty years. That is waning now. Any time you're taking on a project that we're not familiar with, we collaborate with more experienced woodworkers in the shop. It's a wonderful way for all of us to learn and work safely in the shop.*

The shop uses a wide variety of tools, including a band saw, a thickness planer, wooden planes, shavers and Japanese pull saws. Like most boat builders, they occasionally have plans to work from but sometimes do not, especially when they are restoring a traditional boat. One of the most important skills they look for in volunteers is the ability to read plans. The other major skill is being able to replicate a part, such as a rib or a beam, when replacement is necessary.

Each year, the shop manufactures a boat, kayak or canoe that is raffled off to help raise money for the organization. There are several other volunteer groups around Long Island that restore or construct traditional and modern vessels. At the Long Island Maritime Museum in West Sayville, volunteers meet at the Frank F. Penny boat shop on

A kayak ready for raffle. *Photo by Nancy Solomon, 2011.*

the museum's grounds, building one small craft wooden vessel annually. The East End Classic Boat Society in Amagansett, founded in 1988, and the Carmans River Maritime Center in Brookhaven also build traditional boats annually that are raffled off to support their operations. We encourage all readers to get involved in these worthwhile projects.

3

CLARKE BOATYARD

Stephen Clarke, Owner
Greenport

While Greenport is now a bustling summer vacation community, it was once the center of maritime commerce and trade on the north fork of Long Island. Carpenter Street in Greenport, a small alleyway off of Front Street, is home to the oldest boat yard in Greenport, starting around 1830 as the site of a menhaden fish operation, an industry that lasted until the 1980s on Long Island. Historically, the yard was the site of the Greenport Basin and Ship Construction Company, which manufactured military boats during World War II, similar to many boat yards on Long Island.

Stephen Clarke, the owner, recalled, "They were building ninety-foot mine sweepers every thirty days. They also built small landing craft at the rate of one every three or four days. It was a twenty-four-hour day, seven days a week operation. 1,200 men worked here." The Clarke family owned and operated the Promised Land Fish Company in nearby Napeague, where menhaden were processed, servicing their boats at the yard.

The yard is one of the places favored by wooden boat builders and large vessels because it has a functioning marine railway that was designed by Crandall Dry Dock in the early 1900s. The company serviced the Long Island Oyster Farms fleet until the Oyster Farms company went bankrupt. Other businesses at the yard included the Greenport Yachting and Construction Company, which designed and built luxury yachts. Over time, the yard has changed greatly, as workers retired and the yard's balance sheet declined. Owner Steve Clarke decided in 1970 "there was

Steve Clarke, owner. *Photo by Juliana Thomas.*

still too many people in the yard. As these men retired, I started buying machinery. You're not trying to replace people, but you're trying to make it more efficient." Today, Anders Langendal leases space for his boat building and restoration company at the yard.

Greenport Yacht and Shipbuilding is considered small for its size. As Clarke explained, "Everything we handle is less than four hundred tons. That makes us a tiny repair yard." Similar yards like the Jacobsen shipyard in Oyster Bay have closed. The yard has three structures on the site. The largest is used to maintain and restore various types of vessels, including ferry boats, commercial and recreational fishing boats, tugboats and government boats. Clarke added, "We handle everything that floats—steel boats, wood, fiberglass boats. We still work on a lot of aluminum boats."

Many boatyards have removed their marine railways; Clarke relies on his to service large wooden boats and steel-plated watercraft. *Photo by Nancy Solomon, 2011.*

The yard employs five men who are highly valued. "You can't work in a place like this without picking up something every day or week. If you don't learn how to do something different—you learn how to do it better." According to Clarke,

> *We work on fishing boats of all sizes and yachts of all kinds. The largest number of boats we handled were commercial fishing boats. There aren't any more because they have been put out of business for one reason or another—I can't speculate—they are just gone.*
>
> *The east end of Long Island supports a historic commercial fishery that has dwindled as a result of many factors including regulations, the high price of fuel, and the cost for maintaining fishing boats. The real reason we don't see them every year is that they just don't have the money to keep them up. They are maintaining them. Whatever has to be done—it's done—no question about that.*

Where many boat yards have removed their marine railways, Clarke relies on his to service large wooden boats and steel-plated watercraft. The railways must be serviced regularly in order to prevent rusting. We are "exposed to wind out of the south and east—a bad combination. Nobody has been able to figure out how to knock the waves down here. We had serious damage in major storms to boats and equipment. A 120-foot boat slammed up against the bulkhead and sunk during Hurricane Bob."

Owner Stephen Clarke has managed the yard since 1973:

> *One thing consistent in all these yards—we're not selling boats—no new boats are coming in and being sold. There are no boat sales operations here. I guess that everyone was doing some building and doing all the repair work they could when they were not building. In 1970, the yard had no sand-blasting machines, no hydraulic paint sprayers, everything was hand tools and small electric tools. Today we have an ultra-high-pressure jet blaster for cleaning steel. It makes water at 30,000 psi = pounds per square foot inch. The water comes out of the blaster at 2.5 times the speed of sound.*

Like other yard owners, Stephen is concerned about the future. "The future of this yard—I can't answer. But the yard is profitable. The biggest problem is simply to have really smart people to work for you. I never considered anything except a career in the menhaden fishing business or something related to it."

4

COECLES HARBOR MARINA

Peter Needham, Manager and Owner Shelter Island

It's not often that you get to hear about the rich and famous when you do this kind of work, so this yard was exciting to document.

Peter Needham grew up in Glen Cove, the son of an aerospace engineer. Needham reminisced,

> *My father had a Rhodes-18, a Celebrity, which is a wooden boat built over in Holland. I had a dingy. One day I found a rowboat that was smashed on the rocks—and I dragged it half a mile down the beach—pulled it out of water—and my grandfather helped put new planks on the bottom and get it back in water. That became my first boat—a little wooden rowboat. We lived on an island in Glen Cove. Since we were surround by water, I was used to water. It was a big part of our lives.*

In 1973, the Needham family decided to buy the historic Coecles Harbor Marina & Boatyard on Shelter Island, a forgotten jewel where traditional fishing boats and pleasure craft once reigned. As Peter Needham recalled, "I don't know where my father got the idea but he came home one day and said, 'Hey kids what do you think of buying a boat yard?' We said it sounds great. We sold everything in Glen Cove, packed up and moved out here and started working."

Peter spent a lot of time on the water, taking sailing lessons, racing small sailboats and rowing around Shelter Island in a small rowboat. As he grew up, Peter learned that "Long Island Sound could be very rough, and I learned

Boaters from Long Island and Connecticut often spend the weekend at Coecles Harbor Marina. *Photo by Nancy Solomon, 2011.*

to appreciate what the water could do to you, and I also learned about boat design." Peter enjoyed all aspects of the water: "I'm interested in both motor and sailboats. I got a well-rounded picture of the yachting scene."

Like other youngsters on Shelter Island, Peter built little boats when he was a kid. "I had a pond nearby—where I took airplane engines and built hydroplanes—stuck these engines on them and set them on pond. I always wanted a toy sailboat when I was a kid, which I never got. But I did build a few pond boats. Nothing major." Peter got the materials "from whatever I could find in my father's scrap bin. And whatever tools they had." Ironically, "I was a terrible carpenter when I was a kid."

After graduating from high school, Peter enrolled at Southampton College, which later merged with the State University of New York, and studied marine biology. When not in school, Peter and his brother "worked in the boat yard summers and winters." According to Peter, they did the worst jobs in the yard. Needham remembered that "the very worst job was an old thirty-six-foot wooden power boat. It had fifty years' worth of copper bottom paint on it. Gus asked us to grind all the copper bottom paint off—in the middle of winter. We were on a creeper—a thing that you slide underneath a car. We used a big grinder, all of the copper bottom dust got all over you—I was covered in red dust. Till this day I can still taste it." Winter jobs included painting the wooden boats and sanding them.

As he got older, Peter got the notion to sail around the world. He bought a lot of books and read about it, but he was missing a boat. Peter couldn't afford much. "I found a one-hundred-year-old schooner sunken on the bottom in Greenport." When he raised the boat, it had pumps on it. Peter purchased the vessel and proceeded to dismantle it and replace all the pieces in it, spending five thousand hours on it, but never completed the project. As Peter explained, "I learned a lot about carpentry and how a boat was put together. By taking the boat apart you could see how you put all the pieces together. You start to understand why things go together, and what their functions are. By making new pieces for the boat, you learned how to use all the tools and machines in the shop."

Needham never did sail around the world. Instead, he sailed up and down the coast—from the Caribbean to Maine. However, he decided to make the yard his home and career. Mentored by Gus Ciacia, the yard's manager, Needham learned from him "not so much about boat building but about working with people. When we bought the boat yard, Gus Ciacia, who had worked in the Greenport shipyard during World War II building boats, was the foreman. Gus mentored me when I first started to learn. His way of teaching was to let me make a mistake, and then point out what was wrong rather than warning me ahead of time." Among the skills he learned was how to caulk a wooden boat, which he considers a lost art, as more boats are made of fiberglass.

Peter's first boat was a fiberglass sailboat based on a design from the Hinkley Company. He spent two years on and off building it for an imaginary Hamptons client. According to Peter, "It turned out to be a spectacular yacht." Needham still owns it. The yacht was supposed to be built for sale, but he got too attached to it. He launched the boat in 1986. Peter recalled that "the boat was the showcase at the yard. People would come down and say they want the hull to be painted just like *Genesis* (the boat), and the rigging and interior to look like *Genesis*. A lot of the things, like colors, started to be called Genesis Blue, Genesis Cream."

As a result of the success of the *Genesis*, Billy Joel learned about Needham and the yard. "I did a twenty-eight-foot 'Downeaster Isle' boat for Billy Joel. It is a traditionally styled lobster boat that I built as a yacht, with a single engine and a deep keel. I named her the *Half Shell*. Billy wanted a bigger boat, so I ended up building the Downeaster *Alexa*—that he sung about—a thirty-six-foot boat from Maine." The Davison shipyard in East Rockaway,

Peter Needham, co-owner of the yard. *Photo by Nancy Solomon, 2011.*

which is also featured in this book, supplied the motor. Needham also built Joel a mahogany speedboat.

When asked to describe what it's like to work with a celebrity, Peter recounted this story:

> *The first time Billy Joel came in, he was all scruffy. I said "Hey" to him—I didn't even know it was him. We built the Downeaster* Alexa. *Billy came down almost every day and looked at every single thing we were doing. Although we were known for our paint and brush work, he said it was too nice. He did not want it like that. He wanted it to look like the paint was just slapped on. It's a tough thing to teach an artist to do sloppy painting.*

Joel continues to use the boat today.

Peter Needham continues this tradition, building the thirty-eight-foot *Shelter Island Runabout*, launched in 1996, and the thirty-foot *Nomad*, launched in 2008. Both were designed by Doug Zurn from Marblehead, Massachusetts. Along with building the boats, Peter must teach his customers navigational skills and boat maintenance. Peter's wife, Kathi, and brother John manage the boat yard, boat building shop and marina, which includes a swimming pool, picnic area and other amenities. Peter remembers that in the beginning the marina did not have a pool and was not attractive to families coming from Connecticut and other harbors. By installing the pool and picnic tables, a barbecue and a shop where boaters could buy groceries, the marina became more successful. They also added bathrooms and showers.

When I asked Peter Needham about the most unusual request from a customer, he shared this story:

> *There was a young guy from Manhattan—in his early thirties—who knew nothing about boats. He saw a small clip of our boat on News12 (a cable television station) and he loved it. He wanted one. He had zero boating experience. I had to explain what a bow, stern, deck, GPS and teak were. When it came time to making decisions about the equipment, he said, "Check off everything a nice boat should have and then go over it."…I didn't meet him until the day the boat was launched. Together we drove the boat back to Manhattan—because the insurance company didn't let him run the boat by himself. I found him a captain to teach him how to boat. This guy didn't know anything about water, boats—that was very interesting. Needham hired a captain, who is always there. They never got into any trouble.*

Like many boat builders, Peter has a deep appreciation of design and details. While his customers appreciate the overall appearance of his craft, Peter and his staff value the fine details that are part of his boats.

> *Any boat is a collection of ideas from what's seen on other boats. I have been in so many boat yards, when I saw an attribute, and really liked that detail, it ended up in our boat. Boats in this area—not too many to draw from—we have come out of classic New England. We're always critically looking at design elements of the boats on the dock—and asking, "Is the scale correct?" The most important qualities are how it functions and how it rides. The most important thing, to have a good ride in a boat, is it should be fun. Our boats are light, and I enjoy that.*

Coecles Harbor Marina is perhaps one of the few yards included in this book that will survive in the future, as more people look to the water for their rest and relaxation. Needham has a modest but stable staff and is able to both run the marina and work on boats. Peter's children are avid sailboat racers, and he goes to their regattas when time allows. Let's hope the yard continues far off into the future.

5

DONN COSTANZO

Boat Builder and Restorer
Aquebogue

Donn Costanzo is the founder of Wooden Boat Works and current owner of Avery's Boat Shop, where he builds and restores traditional recreational sailboats and motorboats. Raised in Sayville, Donn first became interested in skiffs and garveys, which were used on Great South Bay by local baymen. At the age of seven, "I built a raft with a friend. My father had a bunch of plywood and some Styrofoam. We bolted the Styrofoam to the plywood with my father's help." When he was twelve years old, Donn built a built a rowboat/skiff together with his friend Allen Shortell. Allen used to do all the rowing. Like other young boys in Sayville, Donn would go treading for clams. "I used to put bets up at the Shoreham—a club next door to our house—that I could out row anyone with a motorboat."

As a high school senior, he worked with Al Terry to restore one of legendary boat builder Gil Smith's skiffs, launching Donn on his career path.

> *I was on Fire Island when I saw a boat Al Terry from Bayport had restored—it was a B Class Gil Smith named* Melody. *I wanted to know where I could get one. I talked to Al Terry about the boat, and he asked me all these questions that kids don't ask themselves. He was very kind and extremely patient. He dissuaded me from buying this boat. Instead, he suggested that I restore an old gaff-rigged sloop in his backyard called* Salty. *He suggested I restore that—then I could sail it and use it. Al Terry knew I didn't have the money or resources but had the interest. To him that was all that was important.*

Al would come by when Donn had questions. As Donn recalled in 2012,

> *I reframed it. I put a number of planks and a new deck on the boat, and a new canvas. First and foremost—it's important to know how to look at a boat. You have to get as far from the boat as possible—whether there's a sheer, whether there is a hump, whether the sheer is sweet, whether it's a three-quarter sheer or half a sheer—you are able to tell but only at a distance from the boat. You want to see the boat from the stem to the stern. You also need to walk around the boat. Is the boat twisted at all? Structurally has the boat been tweaked at all, out of shape at all? If it was, immediately you would know where the problems were. From an early stage—Al taught me yacht surveying. When I was done, I spent the summer sailing it, which I did for several years. It was a lot of fun, and I learned a lot. I basically taught myself to sail.*

Costanzo followed a path taken by many young men who grew up on the water, attending college for one year and returning to clamming afterward for six years. During this time, he learned to fiberglass garveys and skiffs used by local baymen in the area. However,

> *It was not until I went to Lance Lee's apprentice shop that I learned classical boat building. At that point, I felt I had some skill that was marketable. What I learned most in the apprenticeship was to be resourceful. It wasn't so much technical. I definitely learned how to plank on frame, learned to loft, but what I really learned was a sense of resourcefulness. I felt that there wasn't anything I couldn't do. If something broke, I could fix it. If you couldn't buy it, I could make it. I came away with confidence. That was valuable to me.*

He later worked in Europe both building and restoring boats.

Donn spent two years in an Italian boat yard restoring a traditional boat, *Sheevra*, that was designed and built by William Fife for himself in 1921. "I got the feeling she had some problems and could possibly be for sale. A friend—the first mate off the *Puritan*—we bought it together and sailed it to Porto Santo Stefano, a picturesque coastal village in Tuscany. We spent two and a half years restoring her—it was a complete restoration—from the keel up. We gained a reputation after the restoration of that boat." They were hired to work on other historic vessels, including the *Belle Adventure* and later the *Altair*—a 109-foot schooner. They sailed the *Altair* to England, where

Donn Costanzo at the Hanff Boat Yard. *Photo by Nancy Solomon, 2012.*

they restored it for two years and sailed it for a year. This enabled him to complete the *Sheevra*, which he also raced. As both an experienced sailor and boat restorer, Donn learned that his combination of skills made him more valuable to other boat owners of classic and contemporary racing boats. As Donn reflected, "At the end of regatta season, somebody would ask you to come and help with the restoration. People saw that we were doing it and thought that one didn't have to have bags of money to go sailing. You don't have to have a ninety-footer, you can have a forty-five-footer. Some money helps, but you don't have to have a huge bank account."

In 1994, Costanzo returned to Long Island, where he has remained. One of the reasons he returned was to fill a gap created by the aging of older boat builders on Long Island. At first, he worked on restoring Beetle Cats, a popular racing boat on Long Island during the 1950s. "We started with one Beetle Cat. Now we have forty," he recalled in 2012. Shortly afterward, Wooden Boat Works began restoring Gil Smith boats and building a John Atkins–designed lapstrake skiff. Eventually, he was able to establish Wooden Boat Works at the Hanff Boat Yard in Greenport, where he could work on larger boats that required deep water. Costanzo worked with several people, including Steve Lubitz, and established builders like Anders Langendal.

"The reason customers come to us is because we have a level of appreciation for the aesthetics of yachts." *Photo by Nancy Solomon, 2012.*

Donn Costanzo inside one of the yachts he restored. *Photo by Nancy Solomon, 2012.*

There are challenges that Costanzo and other boat builders and restorers face, particularly the availability of appropriate wood.

> *It's getting more difficult to purchase timber—particularly boat building timber. Most of the timber coming out of Africa is getting difficult to get and it's expensive. For boat building you have to use the species of wood that does the best job. You are not going to put oak on a deck—it's not going to work out very well with sunlight. You want wood to expand and contract the least. So that decks don't open up during hot weather and leak when it rains. The price of material used to be cheaper than the price of labor—that's changing rapidly. A box of screws costs double to what I made four years ago. Materials are becoming more and more precious.*

Despite these changes, there are advantages to building and restoring wooden boats. "Things get here quicker. It's more expensive for materials but I can do better work now. There are great schools like the International Yacht Restoration School in Newport, Rhode Island." There is also a greater appreciation for wooden boats, one of the key reasons Costanzo can survive. Donn reflected, "I never had a customer who wanted new technologies on the boat—the reason customers come to us is because we have a level of appreciation for the aesthetics of yachts and the technical ability to do it as it was done before."

6

HANFF BOAT YARD

Greenport

When I first came to Greenport to learn about Donn Costanzo and Wooden Boat Works, I learned that they were located in a historic boat yard. The Hanff Boat Yard is owned by John Costello, where they build barges and care for historic wooden boats and modern fiberglass and steel boats, both recreational and commercial. The yard has a long history. In the late 1800s, it was owned by boat builder John Wesley Ketchum, who built two of the marine railways and various buildings, including a boat shop that remains today. According to Hanff's daughters, "You couldn't put a wooden boat in a sling without crushing it. So all of them still came to the boat yard because we had railways. He (our father) put in a second railway to accommodate bigger boats. We were in high school when that second railway was put in—in the 1950s."

In the early 1900s, Bill Hanff and his father began fishing commercially and building docks at local yards. In 1934, the Hanffs decided to purchase the yard, preferring land work to fishing. As their daughter Charlotte Mullen recalled, they realized that they "couldn't build docks forever." Charlotte and her sister Greta Scanlan grew up at the yard, going clamming and crabbing in the waters near Greenport and Coecle's Harbor. Their father went eeling, and their mother was known for her clam chowder, a common dish on Long Island. As Charlotte and Greta remembered, "Growing up out here during the '50s was as close to perfection as we will never find again."

The yard employed many types of workers, including local residents and Norwegian immigrants like the Hanffs, who worked as carpenters.

The Hanff Boat Yard in Greenport. *Photo by Nancy Solomon, 2012.*

According to Charlotte Mullen and Greta Scanlan, "They (the workers) were as rough and tumble as they used to come. They quietly did a lot of good things for a lot of people who remembered as they grew older. People would bring down things to be sanded and for all kinds of stuff, and he (our father) just did it."

They constructed party fishing boats, commercial fishing boats, barges, recreational cruise boats, ferries and other watercraft, using traditional wood framing methods along with modern steel technology. They used a traditional steam box to build the wooden vessels. As the Hanff sisters remembered, "We maintained and serviced cruise boats—people that went out on Sundays—like us. All the small fishing boats from Montauk and the draggers came to us. As years went by, (other yards) went to slings. But you couldn't put a wooden boat in a sling without crushing it. So all of them still came to the boat yard because we had railways. We got new people because we had railways. My father put in a second railway to accommodate bigger boats."

The Hanff Boat Yard was known for its dedicated customers, who regularly came to the yard to talk and socialize. Bill Hanff routinely provided coffee to the staff and any customers who came by and often provided services to the community. They built a pulpit for the Lutheran

The Hanff house. *Photo by Nancy Solomon, 2012.*

The yard attracted a small group of regulars every day. *Courtesy of Charlotte Mullen.*

The winch house at the Hanff Boat Yard with Donn and Bruce Costanzo. *Photo by Nancy Solomon, 2012.*

church in the shape of a whaling ship bow. As the Hanff sisters recalled, "A lot of people would come down—because he (my father) was easy to talk to. He didn't judge anyone. One time someone came in with a broken-down rowboat and he fixed it up and they could have it. He did a lot of good things quietly for a lot of people who remembered him as they grew older."

John Costello was also born in Greenport, the descendant of Irish and German immigrants. "I've worked on the water my entire life. I've been dock building for forty-nine years, starting in late 1962. We bought tugboats down here to get serviced." Costello recalls that there was always a mixture of fishermen and yacht owners at the yard. As a young boy, he shucked scallops and went clamming. Today, he works mostly on barges used for various projects on the seacoast. Maintaining the railways is also challenging, since the wood has to be imported from South America. "I spent a lot of time underwater" installing the posts. The Hanff Boat Yard has an original preserved winch house that is used to haul boats onto the marine railways.

When the Hanffs were ready to sell,

> *My brother and I* [the Costellos] *approached them. They sold it to us for considerably less money than what the developers were offering. We found*

> *a lot of unique old things that most places wouldn't have like ice saws. Costello Marine Contracting business as it is now is a good size company. They made it as easy as possible to buy the place, so long as I kept it operating as marine business. We all have salt water in our blood. I will remain in it for the rest of my life.*

Although John Costello owned the yard in 1992, Bill still worked on various projects. "He liked the groups that came to the boat yard. Every day they would pile in the truck in the back and went to get coffee. They continued to do that till the bitter end—even when they weren't operating as a boat yard anymore. What he liked most about the boat yard were the people that came in—especially the young people." The Hanff sisters are occasional visitors, as they explained: "We go back to the yard whenever John has events. He had fish fries to raise money for his brother's skating rink. The place is always open—you can waltz in there any time."

7

IDA MAY PROJECT

Oyster Bay

In the early 1990s, the Jakobson Shipyard in Oyster Bay announced it was closing, setting up a community discussion of what would happen to the historic shipyard, the working harbor and the oyster industry. Local residents advocated for a new community center where families and adults could learn to sail, go sailing on a historic vessel and learn about the local ecology. The Waterfront Center was born, drawing thousands of people of all ages to its sailing classes, boat rides and other programs.

One of its first projects was restoring the Christeen Oyster Sloop, which currently serves as its teaching vessel. Shortly after the project was completed, the Flowers Oyster Company retired its historic oyster dredge boat the *Ida May* in 2009. The Waterfront Center needed a larger boat in order to accommodate larger school groups and parties who wanted to cruise on Long Island Sound and the harbor. The new *Ida May* is not a restoration project; the staff and volunteers are building a historic oyster dredge boat from scratch, using traditional methods and a combination of traditional and modern materials. The project's first shipwright was David Short, an experienced shipwright who has worked at the South Street Seaport, Mystic Seaport and other maritime museums. Short was assisted by a dedicated group of volunteers, including Bill Shephard, Clint Smith, Jack Hoyt and Ray Wulff. Bill Shephard volunteered on several boat restoration projects prior to the *Ida May* project. When asked why he got involved in these projects, Shephard replied, "Once they're gone that's

The *Ida May* under construction. *Photo by Nancy Solomon, 2012.*

the end of it. Unless people have an affinity for sea going things, this will all be gone." As former Waterfront Center director David Waldo observed, "Every volunteer brings a different skill set to the project. Some people have built their own boats before. Others never did any type of wood working at this level. We've had amateurs to more experienced volunteers. The shipwright's job is to find people's strengths and put them on that project." Josh Herman took over from David Short in 2013, shepherding the project in the following years.

As Short explained in 2012, "The focus of my career has been restoration and repair and completing a number of replicas or reconstructions. The *Ida May* project is not a copy of a boat but the likeness of a boat. We're building it in much the same manner as it was originally built with some improvements." In order to accomplish its goal of using traditional materials and methods, the group brought a small sawmill to the site, where they individually selected trees, depending on the task at hand. Shephard used the mill on a regular basis.

Framing a traditional workboat like the *Ida May* can be very challenging. As Short explained,

> *We are employing the same methods used to build a boat one or two hundred years ago. A system of frames and planks makes it work the way it does. If we start to change anything it would be messing with the whole system. We make some improvements—but you can build a traditional hull that can be friendly to work on, durable, lasting hull—we do that with the materials that have always been used. Ben Franklin said to embrace technology—we do where we can and where it makes sense.*

Short went into forests to identify trees that are good for boat building:

> *There are many varieties of species of trees and many different applications in shipbuilding. I scouted out mast material, trees for deck support, oak trees that can make good keels or big structural pieces of the ship. Part of my education was to learn what kinds of woods to use for what purposes—and more importantly was what* not *to use. We don't use red oak for ship timber—it's more porous and has a tendency to rot faster. Although it's very durable and bends well—and it makes nice small rails. We are making the vessel more durable by using heavier construction materials. Every piece of frame has to be shaped on a band saw. The lofting phase comes first so we can mold the individual pieces.*

Shephard reflected, "A lot of the lumber has to be cut to size—because it is used to support the frame and keel. Cutting the wood isn't new but the way they're using it is. It's a much heavier boat—the way they're putting the supports in."

Newer materials used included marine plywood. "We're installing a plywood deck over the deck frame and using metal stanchions to support the ship's bulwark and rails. It's a stronger and more durable deck construction that eliminates so many chances for fresh water to get in." The construction method will also lower maintenance costs in the long term. The project used adhesives, a newer technology commonly used by boat builders.

The *Ida May,* when completed, will be a traditional wood-framed vessel that uses similar materials and techniques to the original, relying on local woods from Long Island such as locust trees, along with northern woods

Above: Andrew Nenchek and Levi Johnson, two of the project's carpenters and shipwright apprentices, installing the bowsprit. *Photo by Nancy Solomon, 2012.*

Left: A volunteer hammers trundles to secure the frame. *Photo by Nancy Solomon, 2012.*

Opposite: Installing the ribs of the boat. *Photo by Nancy Solomon, 2012.*

found in the Adirondacks and Maine forests. The project is scheduled for completion in 2022. As Short explained,

> *If the original fabric and material is there—you can always find clues to how it was originally put together. We're making the vessel more durable by using a heavier construction approach. There is more material—more wood. The hull form is modified slightly to improve her stability characteristics—* [the Coast Guard] *will look more favorable on this hull as a vessel that will carry passengers than the original vessel that was built without any consideration to carry passengers or Coast Guard regulations. Meanwhile the* Ida May *will reflect the best in both traditional and contemporary boat building practices.*

Shephard and other volunteers hope that they will be able to start a boat building school, so that young people and families can preserve these traditional skills. Bill Shephard emphasized, "Unless people have an affinity for sea going things, this will all be gone. We talk about it so other people might get energized and do the same stuff—we hope."

8

KNUTSON BOAT YARD

Dan Knutson, Manager
Halesite

Huntington is on the north shore of Suffolk County, approximately forty miles east of New York City. For centuries, Huntington has been one of the most active waterfront harbors on Long Island. The Knutson Boat Yard has a long history and one of the largest collections of framed historic buildings. When you enter the yard, you could step back one hundred years in time. As of this writing in 2021, the yard is a site of contention within the Knutson family, sadly. For those who happen to find themselves in the historic town, go visit this yard, where you will be instantly transported to the nineteenth century and earlier.

The Knutson Boat Yard is one of the oldest operating yards on Long Island and dates to the mid-nineteenth century. The first yard on the site was the Atkinson Wheeler Shipyard, followed by the Abrams Shipyard, and in 1937 it was purchased by Thomas Knutson, who kept the Abrams name. "My grandfather—Thomas Knutson, his original name was Torkel Knutson. He came from Norway and changed his name at Ellis Island. He came here with nothing at seventeen years old in 1900. He established himself as a man who worked with his hands; he was a great ships carpenter. He worked at some of the boat yards in the Bronx and some other shipyards. He became supervisor and yard foreman," recalled Dan Knutson, the yard's manager.

When Knutson purchased the yard, there was a hotel/brothel next to the yard. According to Dan, he paid more for the hotel than what he paid for

Knutson Boat Yard. *Photo by Anna Mule, 2010.*

the entire shipyard and then tore it down the following week. He believed he couldn't run a business properly with a brothel next to it.

> *Then the Depression hit. He lost his job. He had these ideas of building boats for the Depression-era wealthy. Because wealthy people couldn't have big yachts because we were on the verge of another revolution. Wealthy people and people with means wanted a great sailboat they could sail around that was not too extravagant. But they liked to race these boats. So my grandfather started building large yachts over one hundred feet long.*

"A lot of them were so prejudiced against Norwegians and Italians that my grandfather didn't change the name to Knutson shipyard till much later," recalled Dan Knutson, the third generation to work at the yard. Many of the workers were Norwegians and Italians whose families had worked in Huntington Harbor as boat builders and fishermen. The Knutsons built wooden boats and ships for use in local industries.

During World War II, the yard eagerly began building military boats for the U.S. Navy, Air Force and the War Department, leading to a major expansion in the yard. According to Dan, "The United States wanted the ships built here. So grandfather was able to retain some of those contracts because he had been building larger ships and was very familiar with doing so in the boat yard when he started."

The Knutsons built army patrol boats that were used in Europe and the South Pacific to transport troops and supplies. As Dan recalled, "The yard had three marine railways, making Huntington Harbor one of the busiest ports on the East Coast." They constructed sixty-five-foot air-sea rescue boats for a very simple reason. Knutson said the government was building thousands and thousands of planes quickly but by inexperienced, insufficiently trained factory workers. Planes were crashing all over the place. There was a 20 percent failure rate. The government needed a boat that could handle any sea. They could build planes easily but didn't have many airmen who could fly planes so they had to save these guys. "The submarine chaser was really the workforce and backbone of the U.S. Navy," according to Dan Knutson. When the boats left the yard, they were run to the armory in Brooklyn Navy Yard, where the guns were installed. The boats were then transported to Europe or Asia.

The timeline for building the war craft could vary. If materials were available and easy to get, it would take six months to build a sub chaser, eight months for a tugboat, four or five days for a landing craft, six or seven days for patrol boats or three and a half months to build a sixty-five-foot air-sea rescue boat. They were all wood-frame boats. Boats that got steel

The Atkinson Wheeler Shipyard was followed by the Abrams Shipyard and the Knutson yard. *Courtesy of the Knutson family.*

The Knutsons built U.S. Army patrol boats during World War II. *Courtesy of the Knutson family.*

plating were the landing crafts and army patrol boats, according to Dan Knutson. The yard built over one thousand landing crafts. At the same time, Knutson also built twelve- and fourteen-foot rowboats, mostly for civilian recreational use.

As Dan recalled, "He was the largest employer in Suffolk County. Approximately 1,200 men worked at Knutson's Boat Yard during World War II, many of Norwegian and Swedish background. Thomas's son Arthur also worked in the yard. The yard milled its own lumber, had a carpentry shop and a machine shop." Other boat yards also produced the submarine chasers, including the Freeport Point Shipyard led by the Scopinich family and the Greenport Point Shipyard.

With the increase in suburban residents after the war, there was more demand for leisure boats, including sailboats. Dan Knutson noted,

> *The first K-35 was built in 1952 as a sloop or a catch at the price of $4,800. The catch came with two masts. A couple of yawl versions*

were also built. They built and designed the boats after a post–World War II lull. People wanted larger boats to take their families on. Families were also getting larger. Boating became part of the American family. Much of the population enjoyed boating, because it was easy to do. The sailboat got more expensive when they started adding bigger motors, fancier galleys, brightwork.

One of the yards most popular boats was the K-37, a sailboat that commanded the impressive sum of $16,000 in the 1960s. The wooden boat included self-bailing teak cockpits, stainless-steel rigging and an indoor "head" or bathroom. There was also a two-burner stove and foam rubber mattresses for sleeping, an innovation at that time. The boat was so popular that it was featured in the television show *Let's Take a Trip* starring Sonny Fox. In the mid-1950s, fiberglass began to replace wooden boats, due to ease of maintenance and the less costly manufacturing process. No longer would dozens of boat builders and carpenters be necessary. While demand was still high for expertly designed boats, including wooden elements, fewer men were needed to work in the yard. Dan Knutson recalled that "during the Korean War—the Pentagon called it the Korean Emergency—the yard got more building contracts for smaller, close-quarter boats. The air-sea rescue boats were still popular, and they also built a lot of landing craft."

When Torkel Knutson was approaching retirement, his two sons—John Knutson and Dan's father, Thomas Arthur Knutson Jr.—took over the yard. John ran the yard, removing the marine railways used for hauling the wooden boats for maintenance and upkeep. One marine railway was left to accommodate the owners of wooden boats, who prefer using traditional marine railways instead of hydraulic lift trailers, which have been known to damage wooden boats. He bulkheaded and covered up the other two railways. By the mid-1960s, wooden boats were no longer built at the yard. John Knutson fell ill, and the yard was turned over to Thomas Arthur Knutson, who modernized the yard. The yard was paved, more slips were added and the final marine railway was removed, replaced by bulkheading.

Dan Knutson is the third generation in his family to work on boats, maintaining them with the knowledge that was passed down to him from his father and grandfather. Growing up, he accompanied his father to various sailboat races, from St. Croix to the Bahamas. In the late 1950s, Thomas was the only person who won the race with a boat he built personally. Eventually, the family bought a marina in St. Croix, which they still own.

The Knutsons built a successful line of sailboats in the 1950s and early 1960s, including the K-Yacht series. *Courtesy of the Knutson family.*

He started working for his father at ten years old as a dock boy. Dan collected garbage to make sure it was disposed of properly. In 1971, when Dan was eleven years old, he went on the payroll, earning sixty cents an hour. At the time, the government allowed minors to work only forty hours a week—Dan recalled that he worked sixty or seventy hours but was paid for only forty hours. As Dan recalled, "At twelve, I told dad, 'I work just as hard as these other men here on the dock.'" Dan asked if he could have more money. His father said no. "I spoke to my sister, and she got him to give me seventy-five cents an hour. I was happy with that."

As he got older, Dan wanted to learn a skill, but "I was told I was too young but I felt I had to learn more." Dan left the marina. His older brother Billy had a marina next to the marine center called Sport Boats.

> *Billy did very well, selling boats—he was a very hard worker—the hardest worker in the family at the time—a real go getter. My father set him up in the late '60s. He was doing all the work himself—he needed all the work he could get. So I started working for him. Billy taught me how to work on engines and outdrives, on newer style smaller boats, how to properly paint bottoms. I learned how to sand and paint the bottom of a boat in an hour. I learned how to work on a lot for the motors, carbonators, outdrives, how to prepare for the customers and wax. Billy trained himself really well—I learned a lot from him.*

Today, Dan helps wooden boat owners keep decorative and functional elements intact, using tools and machines that are often older than his sixty years. Yet times are difficult at Knutson's and other traditional boat yards. The most important income for the yard is the money generated by winter storage fees. The yard has thirty-eight slips. With waterfront property commanding a premium, it is a testament to the Knutsons that the yard has survived. The high price of fuel has also affected the boating industry. Despite the obstacles, Dan continues, as his ancestors did before him, preserving wooden boats for future generations.

9

PETER HEINZ

Boat Builder and Retired Yard Owner
East Marion

I work in Port Washington, where one of our local ice cream stores, Douglas and James, had a beautiful picture hanging of a simple wooden boat. When I asked the owner, Doug, where he got the framed photograph, he introduced me to the builder's son, who later encouraged me to contact his father, who lives in East Marion on Long Island's north fork. Here is Peter Heinz's story.

Peter Heinz was born in Brooklyn, just steps away from Gravesend Bay, where he could wander as a young boy and explore the working waterfront. Peter recalled, "You could walk right down the block to the beach. A lot of neighbors were fishermen." His family moved to Hicksville, Long Island, in 1948. While working as a schoolteacher in Bellmore, he opened the Long Island Sound Sailing Center in 1960–61 in Port Washington, where he lived. The yard was located at the corner of Main Street and Carlton Avenue. In 1959, he began renting sailboats across from Louie's Restaurant. The yard was on lower Main Street, across from "Inspiration Wharf" and the Marshall's Marine Hardware store and boat yard, Manhasset Rigging Yard. Heinz repaired fiberglass sailboats that were damaged in local competitions and races. He also sold sailboats, including the Flying Dutchman series built in San Francisco. "Sometimes we would sell a fleet of 'FJs' to the Amagansett Yacht Club. Sometimes to colleges or prep schools." Yet working on the boats could also be cumbersome. Peter learned how to work with fiberglass, which was a new material at the time he opened his yard.

Boat designed and constructed by Peter Heinz. *Photo by Nancy Solomon, 2011.*

Peter Heinz ran a small boat yard and sailing school in Port Washington from 1960 to 1980. *Courtesy of Peter Heinz.*

"I didn't enjoy working on the boat bottoms—sanding the bottoms and all that. You would be breathing in the bottom paint dust, but I'm still here. I enjoyed doing the interior wood working, rigging the boats for racing and trying to get better performance out of them." Heinz also gave sailing lessons and rented sailboats at Louie's Restaurant.

Peter's business did well, as many Port Washington residents had boats. Among the popular activities were sailing regattas, including the Cannonball Regatta, in various boat classes. Not surprisingly, many of the sailors had accidents during the races. "Generally, when you're rounding a turn, when people are converging at the same mark, they would hit one another and put some damage to the boat. Then they would bring it to us for repairs. All the boats were in very small racing classes. They were built light and more fragile than a cruising boat. And they were more susceptible to damage."

Heinz had a steady stream of customers because he was an accomplished racer, and observers would ask him what kind of sailboat he had. "I sold quite a few each year....One year we sold a fleet of FJs to Michigan State University because one of their students used to stop by our shop who was familiar with us. He recommended us to the school. So we were able to sell outside our immediate area."

Peter also insisted on doing the rigging for all the boats sold by his yard. He explained,

> *Yes, when we buy a boat from the builder we tended to rig it ourselves, get our own mast and boom and rigging. Set it up ourselves. It would be more competitive than using the spurs that would come from the boat builder. It gave us an advantage over others selling stock boat from the boat builder. We put on the hardware ourselves, the spurs, rig it ourselves. Which gave a better faster boat and more profit because we were doing all the work ourselves. Rather than just selling a stock boat.*

In the course of his career, Peter managed to work full-time teaching and running the yard after school and on weekends. "The most difficult thing was learning the business itself, trying to survive in a very competitive field. For a long time, I was teaching in the elementary school and working the yards on weekends and summer. Then about seven years afterward I left teaching and it was just full time in the yard. Eventually, I went back into teaching. Running a small boat yard in a recession time was precarious." The yard closed in 1978.

When Peter retired, he moved to East Marion on Long Island's north fork. He decided to build a traditional wooden skiff.

> *It is a traditional skiff you might see on Long Island's south shore, in Chesapeake Bay, in shallow water areas. People wanted a boat they could build inexpensively and simply. I started out making it sixteen foot and then said what the hell—figure I'll add two more feet. Some of the tools I got from my father, like the hand planes. I used bronze screws—I wanted a traditional look so I used traditional materials. Working with wood is enjoyable. Fiberglass is miserable.*

Although Peter had spent most of his time around sailboats in Port Washington, he decided to build a small motorboat because "fishing from a sailboat is a lost cause. You keep getting your lines around your keel and rudder."

The process was simple but lengthy. "I made sketches thinking I was going to build a model first, using a simple layout. I never did build the model—I just went ahead and built it. At first, I built it roughly using Styrofoam sheets. Until we got the look of the boat we wanted. And then I just took it apart and made templates out of the Styrofoam." The skiff is made of mahogany

Peter Heinz. *Photo by Nancy Solomon, 2011.*

Peter uses the boat to go fishing with his children and grandchildren. *Courtesy of Peter Heinz.*

plywood and lumber, wood he purchased at Condon's Lumberyard in White Plains. "I had a yard dolly, which was just a flat trailer with no real suspension—just a solid axle—that I used for moving boats around the boat yard. We used that as a level starting point." Heinz built a jig in order to build a hull upside down. The hull was built on plywood. As Peter recalled, "I started forming the plywood around the jig. After we finished the bottom and the sides, then we constructed the sides and the bottom, which were screwed and glued together. Then we started working on the interior."

Like other boat builders, Heinz prefers using traditional materials. "I used bronze screws because I wanted a traditional look. We also used bronze cleats and oarlocks." Heinz inherited many tools from his father and from the boat yard. However, he decided to buy a table saw from a yard in Delaware.

> *Shipping on the saw would have been very high so I took my truck down to Delaware. I was told that I would have to have it lifted on a pallet so that I could slide it off when I got to New York. Then I was told that I would have to go through all kind of contortions in order to get it into the basement. The saw weighed about six hundred pounds. When I got to Delaware, instead of a low pallet like I wanted, they had it too high, sticking up too*

high on my truck. We finally loaded it onto my truck. On the New Jersey Turnpike, I was coming up to exits for the Lincoln Tunnel. When I opened my wallet, I found I only had a couple of bucks in it, and I didn't have enough for the toll. I had to get off the Jersey Turnpike, and I started looking for a cash machine, which I finally found. I got back onto the Jersey Turnpike, on one of the busy holiday weekends, and finally made it home.

Peter and his son Tom worked on the boat together and were pleased with the final design and features.

Wooden boats like Peter's attract attention. "We get a lot of favorable comments on it. It looks good in the water. We can roll it right onto the beach. Kids sit in it and go snapper fishing. So it worked out well."

Part II

SOUTH SHORE BOAT BUILDERS AND BOAT YARDS

Long Island's south shore is approximately 120 miles long, starting in Nassau and extending to Suffolk County. It is best known for its shallow bay waters and for producing shellfish, a historic industry on Long Island. Many of the yards profiled have declined in recent years, as demand for boats has fluctuated over time, due to the high cost of buying and maintaining recreational and commercial vessels. Yard owners are faced with high property taxes and often sell to real estate developers eager to build waterfront homes and developments. As a result, several yards included in this section have closed and boat builders have sold their property. Despite these challenges, there are important sites and tradition bearers who continue the traditions of past generations. Many boat builders have designed and constructed recreational motorboats, since the shallow bay waters make it difficult for sailboat captains to navigate, especially during tidal changes. Shoaling is also a problem for south shore boaters, and there are constant efforts to dredge at inlets. During the COVID-19 pandemic, demand has increased for boats, a hopeful sign that the region will continue to be noted for its maritime heritage.

10

AL GROVER

Freeport

Written by Regina Feeney and Nancy Solomon

> *My love affair with boats began at the age of twelve. I used to work weekends fishing on the old wooden Verity skiffs. We'd come into an inlet at night when it was all whitewater—there weren't jetties then—and these boats would go right through the breakers just like ducks.*
>
> —*Al Grover, Verity skiff builder*

Al Grover is a legend in Freeport, New York. When I first met him in 1987, he had just entered the Guinness Book of World Records for the first outboard motorboat crossing of the Atlantic Ocean. Despite his fame, he still found time to sit with me to share his story and has continued to be open to my questions. He celebrated his ninety-third birthday in October 2020. Here is his story, as told to me and Freeport historian Regina Feeney over the course of several interviews from 1987 to 2020.

Growing up in a waterfront community shaped Grover's love of the ocean. As a ten-year-old, Grover collected small boats that had broken free from their moorings, and he would repair and sell them. He has fond memories of fishing in an old wooden Verity skiff at the age of twelve. He is good friends with Fred Scopinich, one of the sons of the legendary boat builder. As a high school student, he played in the band at the ceremony when the Army and Navy presented the "E" award for excellence during wartime to the Freeport Point Shipyard, owned and operated by the

The skiff built by Al Grover. *Photo by Nancy Solomon, 2011.*

Scopinich family. Throughout high school, Grover worked as a mate on commercial and charter fishing boats docked at Freeport. He also ran the boat tender at the South Shore Yacht Club. When Grover turned eighteen, he obtained his captain's license and began working for the Viking fishing fleet. In 1946, after graduation, he enlisted in the military; Grover served as a paratrooper in occupied Japan. When he returned to Long Island two years later, he briefly joined his sister Dotty as a performer in Bruce Parker's touring water ski show.

When the time came to find a job, Grover chose to take his chances on Freeport's waterfront, rather than pursue a career in his family's successful music business. He worked several years as a commercial fisherman. In 1950, with the help of his brother-in-law and a GI loan, he purchased property at 195 Woodcleft Avenue that had once been owned by Henry M. Slocum, a maritime inventor and the owner of Slocum's boat yard. The two-story location had a 135-foot frontage, and the building included a huge showroom, storage lockers, mooring docks, workshops and two apartments upstairs, where the Grovers first lived. By 1952, Grover was one of the youngest and most successful small boat dealers on Long Island, selling almost two hundred boats per year. To eliminate customers' wait times, Grover often traveled to out-of-state boat builders and transported boats back to Freeport using his own car and trailer. Al Grover and his friend George Burmester circumnavigated Long Island in fourteen hours and twenty minutes in a seventeen-foot Thompson lapstrake boat and

The Grover Boat Yard was later sold to Dave Bofill. *Photo by Nancy Solomon, 2007.*

thirty-five-horsepower Evinrude motor in 1957. This was the beginning of the "Around Long Island Marathon." The trip was a precursor to his historic transatlantic boat crossing decades later.

Grover's reputation for good customer service extended internationally. In 1965, he sold Finnish millionaire Uno Pikarla a Chris-Craft cruiser that slept six. Prior to that, Grover sold Greek shipping magnate Aristotle Onassis two specially designed cruisers from Chris-Craft. Grover had been a presence at local boat shows since the 1950s. In 1961, he displayed the Freeporter, a style of pleasure boat designed and constructed by the Freeport Point Boatyard. In 1965, he transported a thirty-eight-foot Chris-Craft Challenger ten miles from Freeport to Westbury on a travel lift for the boat show. The trip took six hours. Grover bought 500 South Main Street in 1969 and built Al Grover's High and Dry Marina, one of the largest enclosed marinas on Long Island. The yard is now run by his son Dante Grover.

Although boat sales were 99 percent of his business, Grover did manufacture small fishing vessels. In the 1970s, while boating down Milburn Creek, Grover found a 1927 Verity skiff that had been partially sunk. He purchased the boat and salvaged it. Verity boats were legendary for their seaworthiness, especially in rough weather. Grover recalled a news report of two local fishermen who survived a major storm in a Verity skiff. He also remembered Verity boats overloaded with fish navigating along Freeport's waterways with ease.

Knowing he had found a gem, Grover asked the Chris-Craft factory in Cortland, New York, to make a mold of the skiff for him; he used the mold to produce fiberglass versions of the boat.

> *The Verity skiffs that I copied were boats that I was familiar with in my childhood in Baldwin. I loved Verity skiffs because they were very seaworthy and good in shallow water, and I always wished I could have one as a kid. The only ones I had were junkers, and they wouldn't even float. But there were a lot of them in commercial fishing and I always—like you fall in love with a beautiful girl—you like the shape. The Verity had a beautiful shape. It had a flat spot on the bottom so when you ran aground it didn't turn on its side.*

Grover showcased the boat at the Greater Long Island Boat Show in 1976. The public had little interest in this boat until the U.S. National Park Service for the Gateway National Park ordered one in 1977. Later, the design became popular with south shore fishermen.

Grover displayed another 1920s-inspired Verity skiff in 1981 when the gas crisis and economic downturn put a damper on high-performance boats that ran on gasoline.

> *I went into boat retail, sales and service, and we were doing very well. It was constantly more and more volume each year until somewhere around Nixon or Carter, they started to have a rule that pleasure boats couldn't get gas. As you remember, there were lines of cars trying to get gas at the gas station. You spent half your life trying to get gas to get to work. So, they put red flags up at the marine stations which means no gas for pleasure boats. Next, one of the presidents decided to add a 10 percent luxury tax, so we're already running out of gas, we have 8 percent NY tax and now we have the 10 percent luxury tax, so if a guy is buying a $100,000 boat he's got $18,000 of tax. This slowed us up to the point where our sales were very, very slow and I was looking to do something to stimulate what I thought was a place in the market that nobody was really going into.*

Al was surprised when he started selling and getting orders for the Verity boats he designed and produced in the 1970s.

The guys that couldn't get gas for the big fishing boats or the "Bertram" or "Hatteras" type—they would come down with five-gallon buckets of home heating oil and put it in my little boat and still could go fishing for the day. Home heating oil was fine to burn in the diesel engine most times. So, they could go out and we began to sell a lot of these boats. The other thing that got to me was that I had to prove that it was very seaworthy.

In 1985, Grover, accompanied first by his son Al Jr. and later by son Dante, sailed three thousand miles from Nova Scotia, Canada, to Portugal in a twenty-six-foot "Groverbuilt" skiff named the *Spirit of Freeport* with Evinrude engines.

So, I took my son Al Jr., and we took two boats—he was going to run the second boat and I was going take the twenty-six-footer with the three outboards. His boat also had three outboards. We had two trailers and we were heading to Maine up toward Newfoundland—because Newfoundland is very close to Ireland and England and it's the shortest way you can get across the ocean. On the way up, we had an accident with the towing vehicle on the second boat. It jackknifed and the boat went off the trailer down into a ravine. It was pretty much wiped out. At that point I called my wife and said, "Well, this isn't a very good omen. I quit." We picked up the pieces. We went to a motel. We gathered everything together, and I said we can take one boat and still try to make it.

Grover and his son found their way to Nova Scotia, where they began their journey. "My son and I took off for Europe on August 1, 1985. Of course, that's the beginning of the hurricane season but we had so many delays you get to the point where you say 'now or never.'"

Along the way, Al remembered,

We met a French couple in Saint Pierre and he's on a big sixty-foot sailboat, and he said he would keep in touch with us on our single side band radios. Of course, we're not in sight of each other because he's sailing and I'm powering. So we made out okay for the first ten days, and I decided I would put down the small engine. The small engine didn't have the electric tilt, but the two big engines did so you could tilt them in and out of the water from the pilothouse. However, the smaller engine had to be put down by hand. My son was sleeping so I decided to go out on this six-inch-wide gunnel working my way to the stern, and when I tried to push the engine down, I

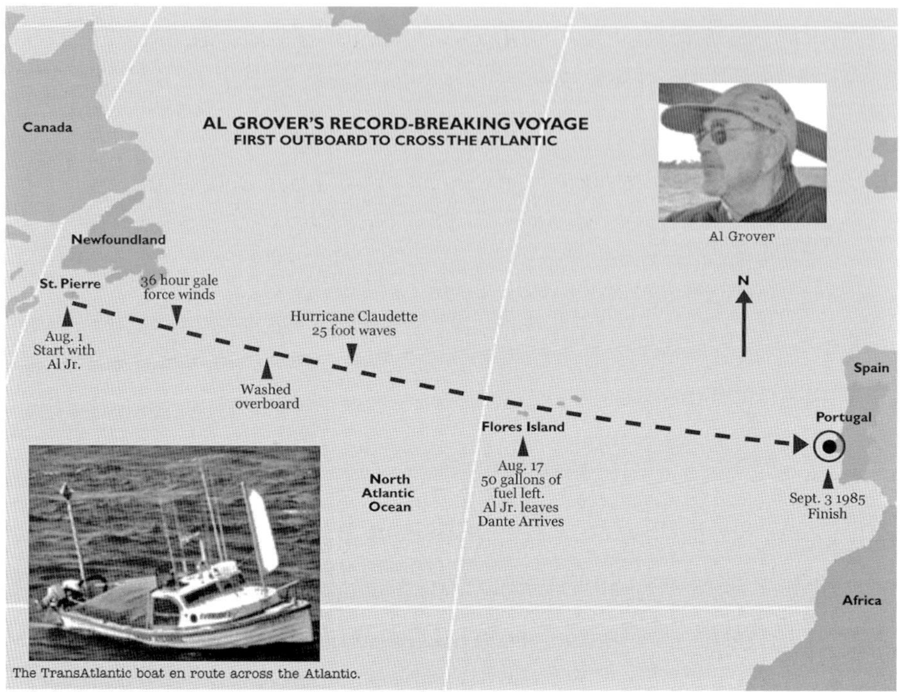

The Grover transatlantic crossing. *Courtesy of Al Grover.*

had forgotten that you must first pull it up and release it, and I kept pushing and pushing hard on it and finally the engine went down but with all my weight behind it, I did a somersault over the back of the boat and when I came up, the boat was sailing away and my son was sleeping in the cabin.

I yelled as loud as I could, and I don't think I woke him up, I think something else woke him up. But he stuck his head out of the hatch and he hesitated, and I said, "You know, he's probably thinking that's a good time to get rid of the old man." But he had to make a very big turn because our engines were locked so that you couldn't steer with the outboards, we were steering with the original rudder, which is underneath the boat. But it didn't make a sharp turn. He didn't want to back on to me because he was afraid I could get messed up in the propellers. So he finally picked me up.

We kept going til the seventeenth day which was August 17, when my French friend called me on the single side band (radio) and said, "We have a problem. There's a hurricane that just cleared someplace in the Caribbean." I thought they all came up the United States, but this one was heading for Europe. And it was heading to the island of Flores which was

> *the first island you hit in the Azores. We hit waves and he was recording seventy-five-knot winds and eight-meter-high waves so we had a couple of bad days. But it calmed down and we made it to the first island of Flores.*
>
> *At that point, my son Al, he had had it. He disappeared as soon as we docked. He took off. I called my wife and I said "I quit. Al is not with me, and the boat is in terrible shape." And she said, "You can't quit. You must finish. Stay there and I'll send Dante over." Dante didn't want to go, but everyone knows my wife is the boss. She said, "You go and bring your father back to Europe." And so Dante flew over to the island and we made it the next eight hundred miles in eight days to Lisbon, Portugal, and that was the end of our trip.*

This trans-Atlantic journey established a world's record. "They (The *Guinness* Book) told me there was no outboard powered motorboat of my size that had made a crossing without help." To honor this feat, the Village of Freeport declared September 22, 1985 "Grover Day" and hosted a parade in honor of the Grover family.

The Grover family has always promoted Freeport's waterfront. Rosemarie "Artie" Grover, Al's wife since 1953, conceived of the name "Nautical Mile" for Woodcleft Avenue in 1965. The Grovers were instrumental in founding SPLASH (Stop Pollution, Littering and Save Harbors) and the former South Street Seaport at Freeport museum. Over the years, Al and Artie Grover have served on many waterfront committees and have worked tirelessly on behalf of the village. They truly are Long Island treasures.

11

JOHN REMSEN SR.

Boat Builder
Freeport

In 1987, I began working in Freeport, documenting local maritime culture for the Long Island Arts Council at Freeport. One of the first people I met was John Remsen Sr., who was the fourth generation of his family to work on the bay. John was born in 1933, and at a young age he was already catching bait fish using handmade killie traps, a skill he learned from his great-grandfather Alanson Ellison. As a youngster, John would surf net using a dory. "I would go with my father in the boat to watch him doing things and that's how I learned." They would often go to a nearby oyster house where the older baymen would tell stories and fix their nets. John would also work with his grandfather all day long and then row home.

John was one of the few men on Long Island who built garveys, a traditional flat-bottom boat used by baymen and recreational fishermen in the shallow south shore waters of Nassau and Suffolk County. During his lifetime, he built over one hundred boats. Like the generations before him, John maintained a traditional way of life. As a young boy, he helped Ellison go haul-seining on the ocean. He also went duck hunting, trapped killies and crabs and fished for fluke and flounder.

When I asked why he started building garveys, John replied, "It was a need and a want that resulted in building a boat. I just wanted a garvey when I was a kid. My father had one built by a professional in Long Beach, and I copied that one. Originally they were all wood boats." This dream became reality when his high school shop teacher, Joe Devlin, encouraged and taught him to build parts for his boat. He made his first boat in 1958.

John Remsen Sr. *Photo by Nancy Solomon, 1996.*

"When I first started it cost $350 for one boat, today (1988) it's $2,500." Since then, the cost has increased to $5,000.

Until the 1960s, the garveys were made of cedar planks and green oak. Remsen used cedar, traveling to New Gretna, New Jersey, to get it and oak from Harned's Sawmill in Commack. "In order to build the boats, we air-dried the cedar at home. We also sawed and planed the edges of the planks.

John worked in his garage and driveway. Shown here are the nearly completed ribs for a garvey. *Courtesy of the Remsen family.*

The oak ribs were bent with steam. We would put a pipe in a fire that would expel steam onto the oak that was placed in a steam box. Each oak rib was typically fifteen to sixteen feet long. Only green oak was used because dried oak would crack." Some of his garveys had low sides for clammers, which made it easier to pull in the rake, while others had high sides for eel harvesters who used traps that were easier to lift. Like other traditional boat builders, John built his boats in his garage and driveway.

John's garveys are distinctive by their design and materials. As he explained in 2016, "I can always pick my boats out. They have a certain style. We put a sweep in the bow. The interior was made according to whoever wanted the boat. If they were clamming they may want a pilothouse, and if they were fishing they may want seats or a console. Usually, I could sell more than I could build." Occasionally, John also built boats for gillnet fishermen who worked in Great South Bay and various east end towns. However, most of his customers lived and worked in Nassau County and Western Suffolk County.

Above: Remsen garveys, 2016. *Courtesy of the Remsen family.*

Left: John Remsen Sr. and his son John. *Photo by Nancy Solomon, 2006.*

John used twenty to thirty forms and patterns he personally designed. He started using fiberglass in the 1960s to make the boats lighter, which eliminated the need for painting and allowed them to be transported by trailer. Upon retirement, Remsen began building garveys with his son John, a part-time bayman, for SPLASH, a local environmental group in Freeport. He received an apprenticeship grant from the NY State Council on the Arts to teach his son the advanced techniques of garvey building. On September 9, 2016, the Village of Freeport honored Remsen for his service to the country and community by naming canal number 4 Remsen Canal behind West Fourth Street in Freeport where Remsen lived. One of John's last projects was to build a large garvey for SPLASH. He passed away in August 2020. Some of the members, including Rob Weltner, one of the principal founders of SPLASH, re-created one of his garveys to replace an earlier one. Weltner added, "So many people loved that boat, and it represents us and it's a beautiful boat. We took the old one apart very delicately and we decided to replicate it. We beefed up a few spots." The boat will be used to help clean the canals.

To continue the legacy, Remsen's son John and his grandsons will continue the tradition, assisted by his cousin Tom Jefferies, a bayman, who also owns one of Remsen's garveys. We hope to see more Remsen-built garveys in the years to come.

12

SCOPINICH BOATYARD

Freeport and East Quogue

by Regina Feeney and Nancy Solomon

Freeport Point Boatyard, later known as the Freeport Point Shipyard, was founded in 1923 by brothers Frederick (1891–1975) and Mirto "Mike" Scopinich (1898–1986) along with family friend and fish dealer Captain John Carcich (1867–1943). The boat yard was located on Woodcleft Avenue, a road paved with clamshells and under development at the time. In 1928, the brothers purchased Carcich's share of the business for $25,000.

This boat yard built many varieties of watercraft, including yachts, police boats, United States air-sea rescue boats and, during World War II, British Royal Navy patrol boats. They also constructed boats for the Lighthouse Service, the Public Health Service and the New York Harbor Patrol. In the 1920s, the shipyard built a number of commercial fishing vessels, including the fifty-foot *Benita* and the *Lindy*. As Fred Scopinich recalls, the *Lindy* fishing boat, launched in 1927, was named after Charles Lindbergh when he crossed the ocean. Throughout the nation, residents cheered young Lindbergh on his adventures. The Scopinich family rented the *Lindy* out to commercial fishermen, including Ilia Zvitcovich, for offshore scallop fishing. The vessel was caught in the 1938 Long Island Express hurricane and presumed lost. Scopinich said, "We assumed it was lost and then heard that the boat was in Brooklyn. The boat was also used for rumrunning."

During Prohibition (1920–1933), Freeport Point Shipyard built fifteen vessels for the Coast Guard and thirty for rumrunners. The shipyard could

The crew at Freeport on an all-aluminum lifeboat in 1941. *Courtesy of Fred Scopinich.*

complete a rumrunning boat in two weeks. Rumrunner boats were outfitted with two or three five-hundred-horsepower World War I–surplus airplane engines and bulletproof pilothouses and engine rooms. To outrun patrol boats, the rumrunners were equipped with a smokescreen device that was connected to the boats' exhaust system. Though registered as fishing vessels, the rumrunners could travel thirty-two to thirty-five miles per hour fully loaded with illicit alcohol. Scopinich built rumrunners, including the *Everett* in 1929; the *Anna B.*, built in 1932, purportedly for the owner of a Hempstead speakeasy; and the *Wanda*, which was later captured by the U.S. Coast Guard. It was alleged that the Freeport Point Shipyard constructed three forty-two-foot rumrunners capable of transporting four hundred cases of alcohol for notorious bootlegger Dutch Schultz. The Scopinich brothers built the *Maureen* in 1931; it was able to avoid capture for the duration of Prohibition. Ironically, two years after Prohibition's repeal, *Maureen*'s sister ship, the *Mona Lola*, grounded at Jones Beach, leaving as many as nine hundred cases of Cuban liquor strewn along the beach.

Fred Scopinich remembered his excitement at going to the yard during this time: "I grew up in the boat yard—every day I would watch what was going on. There was nothing else I wanted to see except what the next day's progress was going to be." His memories of the rumrunners are clear, even today in 2021. According to Fred,

> *The boat* Maureen *took five crew members out of the inlet. They got out to the Coast Guard boat that was patrolling the inlet who stopped them and asked where they were going. They told them they were going mackerel fishing. As they said this, two fellows jumped off the boat with pistols and held up the Coast Guardsmen. They stayed in the Coast Guard boat and the other boat went out, got its load of rum, went in and unloaded. Afterward the rum running crew sent a skiff out to pick up the two guys. The two guys who held them up hid $200–$300 in the boat and told the Coast Guardsmen, "If you report us we're reporting you that you took a bribe."*

Ultimately, Prohibition led to improvements to marine design and production in Freeport. Pete Budinich and John Marinzulich purchased two draggers from Freeport Point in 1934, the *Polaris* and *Niram*. They were used as shrimp boats in South Carolina during the winter. In 1938, the shipyard built two forty-five-foot double cabin air-sea rescue patrol boats with a *V*-type bottom and outfitted with four-hundred-horsepower motors. The

This rumrunner was one of twenty-five built during Prohibition. *Courtesy of Fred Scopinich.*

mahogany-trimmed boats, with a traveling speed of forty to forty-two miles per hour, were delivered to the Brooklyn Navy Yard.

To ensure Freeport Point was awarded its regional share of government boat contracts, the shipyard appointed Judge Hilbert Johnson as an officer in 1925. Johnson, a first-generation American, was a much-respected politician and local personality. Johnson's support helped bring prestigious maritime contracts to Freeport.

After Prohibition was repealed in 1933, the rumrunner fast-boat design became popular with the U.S. Navy. In the years that led up to World War II, the Freeport Point Shipyard began construction of patrol boats, crash boats and buoy boats for the U.S. Army and Navy. The yard was awarded the Army and Navy "E" award, given to war plants for excellence during wartime. Due to the high volume of wartime production, the Village of Freeport gave the shipyard two temporary shelters to store the lumber and government-furnished engines in 1943. At the beginning of the United States' participation in the war, Freeport Point employed between fifty-six and seventy men. By the close of the war, employment decreased to a dozen. Freeport Point's $280,000 government contract was believed to be the largest boat building contract awarded to a company located in Nassau County.

One of the first boats constructed after the war was the forty-five-foot trawler named *Sturgeon*, purchased by Freeporter and commercial fisherman Ben Bracco. In the 1960s, the Scopinichs designed and built a thirty-two-foot pleasure cruiser known as the *Freeporter*. One of the largest pleasure crafts constructed by Freeport Point Shipyard was a sixty-five-foot yacht for Nicholas Goulandris, a Greek shipping magnate. The shipyard also built a fifty-two-foot motor sailboat that was shipped to Venezuela. In 1961, the shipyard built twenty boats ranging in size from thirty-two to thirty-seven feet. In the 1960s, the shipyard constructed a twenty-eight-foot skiff based on the rumrunner design named the *Columbia II*. In 1965, the shipyard launched two sixty-five-foot ferry boats. One was named the *G-Whiz*. This was the first ferryboat constructed at the yard. The $130,000 ferry included three 6-110 General Motors diesel engines with a combined horsepower of 945 and had a capacity of 150 passengers. It took five months to construct.

Joseph C. Scopinich (1926–2007), Mirto's son, worked as the shipyard's mechanical engineer. He helped design and build boats for the New York Police Harbor Unit and two ferries that carried passengers to Fire Island. When Fred's father and uncle decided to sell the yard in 1956, Fred and his

The Fire Island *Dutchess* sixty-five-foot passenger ferry built 1966. *Left to right*: Mario Scopinich, Ken Stein, Fred Scopinich Sr. and Fred Scopinich Jr. *Photo by Joseph Adams; courtesy of Fred Scopinich.*

brother Mario bought the Hampton Shipyard in East Quogue, which was abandoned at the time. The Hampton Shipyard dates to the late 1800s. They began building twenty-eight-foot wooden Columbia recreational fishing boats. As Fred Scopinich recalled, "Most of our boats went to

Fred Scopinich. *Photo by Nancy Solomon, 2021.*

Freeport and Mystic, Connecticut. One of the main differences between building for the military and individuals was that you did not have to meet military standards that were inspected. You could use your own knowledge and improve." Today, Fred's son and grandson help local wooden boat owners maintain their craft, through restoration and maintenance, while continuing to build the famed Columbia Cruisers. The last Columbia Cruiser was built in 2021.

13

MARESCA BOAT YARD

199 Woodcleft Avenue, Freeport

Written by Nancy Solomon and Regina Feeney

Walk along Freeport's "Nautical Mile" today and you will be hard pressed to recognize it as the former fishing and boating capital of Long Island. Gone are the days when you would see a dozen commercial fishing boats, an equal number of party boats and dozens of charter boats. Today, Woodcleft Avenue is dominated by restaurants and bars, with few reminders of its nautical heritage. One exception is the former Maresca Boat Yard, which now serves as the headquarters of SPLASH, a local environmental organization that sponsors clean-up activities using traditional garveys.

Maresca's Boat Yard was located at 199 Woodcleft Avenue. It was run first by Phillip, with his sons Phil, Tony and Everett. The Maresca family moved to Freeport in the early 1920s, and Phillip Sr. worked as a printer and house builder. When the Depression struck, Phillip began building boats full time; the vessels he built included trawlers and other commercial fishing boats, which were in high demand in Freeport. In 1927, Fred Scopinich, who owned the Freeport Point Shipyard down the street, built a boat for Phillip, demonstrating the camaraderie among the boating community in the village. Phillip went on to build several boats of his own.

Like many Freeporters during Prohibition, Maresca may have supplemented the family income as a rumrunner. A scallop boat he owned called the *Hercules* was seized on Rum Row offshore and sank as it was towed back to shore. Maresca maintained that it sank because the Coast Guard had

The Maresca Boat Yard circa 1950 on Woodcleft Canal. *Courtesy of Jerry Maresca.*

used it for target practice. During the Great Depression, the family moved to Suffolk County and started a boat yard in Hampton Bays. In 1938, Maresca returned to Freeport in a boat constructed by Phillip Jr. and established a boat yard on Woodcleft Canal. He had an additional yard on Hudson Canal.

The Maresca family, of Italian heritage, hired eastern Europeans to work in the yard. Jerry recalled "they were craftsmen. The carpenters came from Trieste, and many worked there for quite a few years. Mostly it was family." When Phillip Maresca died in 1941, his three sons took over the business, which they ran for forty-one years. Everett Maresca remembers that he always went to the yard while he was growing up. "You grow up fast when you're working with your family," Everett recalled during a 1990 interview. He learned several things from his father: how to refinish wood boats, how to paint the bottoms and how to notch and rivet the planks for large wooden boats. Everett would later pass these skills on to his sons, including Jerry. They were taught to never waste anything. "They used to straighten nails out, stir the bottom of the paint can to get every last drop. Nothing was ever wasted," recalled Jerry Maresca. Most of their business centered on repairs to large boats. They purchased much of their wood from upstate New York and out of state. Maresca used mahogany for planking and oak for framing.

Everett Maresca, circa 1952. *Courtesy of Jerry Maresca.*

Around 1968, Everett Maresca constructed a large facility where boats could be refurbished indoors year-round. In the early 1970s, Maresca's Boat Yard serviced three to four hundred boats per year. These included commercial fishing boats, draggers, charters and yachts. Notable boats they worked on included the *Apache*, owned by the Cona brothers; *Roslyn Sea*; the *Bozo*; the *Skimmer*; and the *Trade Winds*.

The yard serviced the party boats that were part of the Freeport Boatmen's Association, located across Woodcleft Canal from the Maresca boat Yard. In the late 1960s and early 1970s, there were several hundred party boats in Freeport, according to Everett. As Jerry Maresca recalled, "You could go from mahogany speedboats all the way up to Chris-Crafts, and everything in between. It was a lot of different types of boats." Their work including planking, hulling and bottom painting to meet Coast Guard inspection standards.

One of Maresca's most famous clients was band leader and racing boat competitor Guy Lombardo. The brothers were mechanics for Guy Lombardo's speedboat Tempo VI. Jerry did the bottom painting as a teenager. Jerry recalled,

> *One time, Lombardo was heading into the city and he had the* Tempo *in the slings. I was touching up the paint. He came down and bent over and asked, "How's it going, kid?" He kind of startled me. And with the flick of the brush I got bottom paint all over his suit. Then my uncle came out and started screaming at me, "You dopey kid, what are you doing?" Guy Lombardo said, "Leave him alone, I startled him. I have plenty of other suits, I'll go home and change."*

Jerry Maresca and his brothers also grew up learning the trades of their father. As Jerry recalled in a 2016 interview, "Eight family members

Guy Lombardo (*driver*), circa 1962. *Courtesy of Freeport Historical Society.*

worked there. There were another eight to ten workers in addition to family. This was my first job. In the early 1960s, there were only wooden boats. Fiberglass began in 1968. I was born in 1950. I was eleven years old when I first started working at the yard. It was an apprenticeship. Later I learned to block boats and how to run the lifts." The Maresca family also built and modified more traditional boats such as garveys, skiffs and duck boats, which they also used personally.

The Maresca Boat Yard operated until the late 1970s. In 1997, the sixty-nine-thousand-square-foot site of the Maresca Boat Yard became the South Street Seaport Museum's Long Island Marine Education Center. It was leased by the Village of Freeport to the South Street Seaport for one dollar a year. Today, the site is the headquarters of Operation SPLASH (Stop Polluting, Littering and Save Harbors).

14

THE HARTER BROTHERS

Bellmore

Commercial fishing was once a thriving industry on Long Island, dating to the colonial period when whaling ports dominated Cold Spring Harbor, Sag Harbor and Greenport, among other coastal communities. Growing up in Bellmore, Rob and Ron Harter spent much of their youth fishing and boating. The brothers built their first boat, a small five-foot wooden plank boat, when they were nine years old. The two brothers were enthralled with the bay, going there after school. When they got older, they bought a fourteen-foot kit boat from Sears and Roebuck, which they assembled themselves. They launched their boat from nearby Wantagh Park, formerly known as Seabreeze Park. By the time they were in their twenties they graduated to Chris-Crafts and other recreational boats.

As Rob recalled, "I always wanted to go commercial fishing. Ronny my brother always talked about how he wanted to build a boat. In *National Fisherman* there were study drawings of this forty-three-foot boat. It was a steel boat designed by Bill Ohrle from Massachusetts. He was almost in his eighties when he finished that design."

Their first fishing boat was the *Puffin*, a forty-three-foot boat weighing twenty-five thousand pounds, constructed in 1984 in Ron Harter's backyard in Ronkonkoma. Ron was a certified welder by the Coast Guard. The boat was finished and launched in West Sayville. After that, they built "a couple of barges for dock builders." The brothers quit their jobs in 1991, a time when commercial fishing was still a viable occupation, to become full-time commercial fishermen and boat builders.

The *Puffin* harvested fluke, flounder and squid. *Courtesy of the Harter family.*

Their next vessel was the *North Sea*, built from famed Scottish builder Maurice Napier's designs. According to Rob, "His big thing was the stability of vessels and fishing vessels—he was known all around the world as a fishing vessel designer, as well as ferries." Napier visited the *North Sea* on several occasions, and when completed, he commented, "You built it exactly as I wanted, and you did a great job."

> *We thought it was within our means to build something along the line of the* Seth Green*—but we built it one foot heavier, one foot wider, and one foot deeper. It weighs 200,000 pounds when fishing. Which is extraordinary. There's no other fish boat like the* North Sea *on the whole East Coast. I challenge anybody to say they have anything as good as that boat in that size. It's impossible. It's an awesome boat with an awesome design. Anybody who fished with a good boat, who took pride in the boat, they all felt it was a friend of theirs, even though it's an object. It had a life with a soul.*

Like the *Puffin*, the *North Sea* was used to harvest squid, yellowtail and flounder. The Harter brothers often went as far as one hundred miles from

The *Puffin* and the *North Sea*, circa 2004. Fisherman Timmy Swanson of Freeport purchased the *Puffin*, renaming her *Li'l St. Pete*. *Courtesy of the Harter family.*

the Shinnecock dock, in winter and summer. "Traditionally a guy could make his day if he had ten carts of flounder, a couple cartons of squid and a couple cartons of butterfish. By the end of the day, he had a decent amount of money from a little bit of this and that," recalled Rob Harter.

The *North Sea* was a successful fishing boat until the passage of the 1995 Magnusson Stevens Act, which began a series of fishing regulations that

Ron Harter (*left*) and Rob Harter circa 1992, when the *North Sea* was under construction. *Courtesy of the Harter family.*

severely restricted the industry, including Long Island's fishing fleet. "You can't combination fish anymore because of the way the rules are—you have to target certain species." Ron Harter explained that

> *the whole thing went from being somewhat reasonable to being ludicrous—where you can't work anymore and guys couldn't have any bigger boats. The whole complexion of fishing changed—it basically took me out of the business of building because nobody could build anymore. These guys made an empire of fishing rules. They just went wild. Who are they saving the fish for? Nobody can get them. I don't know who is supposed to get them. It's not like you opened up an off-track betting parlor. It was an honest living.*

Faced with the new regulations, they sold the *North Sea* to fisherman Billy Reed of Hampton Bays and the *Puffin* to Timothy Swanson of Freeport. Both boats are still working.

15

DAVISON'S BOAT YARD

East Rockaway

In 1932, Russell Davison founded a yard that specializes in boat building, restoration and service along the shores of East Rockaway. He had two sons and a daughter in the business—who Dan Schmidt, the last owner, eventually purchased the yard from. "Ken Cot was the manager and mechanic. Oliver Davison was the engineer and ran all the equipment. They manufactured anything you needed to make. Russ was the painter and carpenter. They were a good match because they all had different skills." The yard was well known for building and servicing commercial fishing boats and luxury yachts, Coast Guard skiffs and police boats. It was among the oldest working boat yards on Nassau County's south shore.

The Davisons lived in what is now the office, which was originally a barge thought to be built in the late 1800s. Dan Schmidt recalled,

> *It was a working barge—like coal barges in Brooklyn—out of service—the bottom was all rotted out. Back then it was where the men worked and lived. Russ bought this property, but he needed to live here. The house movers didn't want to build a house on the property. So Russ found and bought a barge. He lived on the water for two years. Then Doris (his wife) came home one day and it was up on land. They lived a couple of years on land. Then Davison lifted it in the air and built what is underneath it. We are sitting in his office that was added on later. Residence upstairs.*

The yard had several historic buildings when I visited in 2011.

"The shanty" in the mid-1940s. *Courtesy of Dan Schmidt.*

"Years ago, there were painters, welders, different levels of carpenters. We had fine carpenters who did varnish work. Then there were 'nuts and bolts' carpenters—they had to put seams together, caulk a boat and put lapstrakes and rivets back in. The woodworkers came from Scandinavian countries," recalled Dan Schmidt. The yard worked on Coast Guard boats, fishing party and charter boats and the local police harbor patrols. Most of the workers stayed with the yard for over ten years.

Over time, the yard expanded its services to include dealer training on Mercruiser motors and maintaining "party" fishing boats such as the *Commodore*, the *Genie May* and the *Captain Tom*. While motorboats were more common during the yard's beginnings, sailboats were also part of the yard. "Oliver and Russ were sailors—they would buy sailboat hulls—bring them here and would put them together. They would sail the boat, use it, sail it and build another one."

"I worked every Saturday and Sunday. Years ago—the men would meet with Davison's and find out what's wrong with their boat—it was a man's type

The main structure of Davison's Boat Yard. *Photo by Nancy Solomon, 2013.*

of organization. Most of the time women never went on the boat." When I met Schmidt in 2011, he said, "Today we're not even open on weekends. Everyone is busy with their family. Now the wife comes down too. If you were a boater years ago, you were a boater that did other things."

Dan Schmidt was the last owner of the yard. "I got started in the early 1970s—my parents had an older wooden boat that they kept at Davison's. When I was a teenager, I started as a part-time employee in the summertime. In ninth or tenth grade I decided to spend the summers working at the yard. After high school, I became a full-time employee." As Schmidt explained, "This is a unique industry—no one goes to school to become a boat yard guy. You have to learn the long, hard way."

Dan Schmidt began working at Davison's in 1976. "I started as a part-time employee in the summertime. Things were much harder since most boats were wood." During this time, Schmidt worked on a variety of boats, including those manufactured by the Wheeler, Matthews, Chris-Craft and Pacemaker brands. Like Russ Davison, Schmidt worked with many of the same people for many years. "All the craftsmen knew each other and would share with each other. I remember doing that with Fred Scopinich also. We're in business with each other as well. We realized the customer moved around and realized that it was everybody's customer. We worked well together in those days. You still see that locally in the trade—to help each other out."

Jim O'Reilly began working at Davison's in the 1960s. *Photo by Nancy Solomon, 2013.*

In previous years, each boat yard had its own mechanics, painters, woodworkers and carpenters. Today, most tradespeople work in a variety of yards, on contract, so that they can work year-round. One of the exceptions was James O'Reilly, who owned Sandpiper marine, a paint and carpentry shop on the Davison's yard. Jim O'Reilly began working at Davison's in the 1960s. After leaving to run his own boat yard in 1980, he retired and returned to Davison's.

Occasionally, Schmidt and Davison had to educate their customers on what was feasible and desirable in boat design.

> *People have visions of something that's not right. One customer bought this boat with a diesel engine and wanted to put a stern drive package on back of the boat. I looked at the job and quoted a price, but it wasn't made to do that and can't make that boat do that. The customer would question… my ability—but it's like taking a four-wheel car to make a three-wheel car. I can't put my name on it. It will never be right. Run into that quite often.*

In 2012, Superstorm Sandy flooded all of Davison's buildings, swept boats off their stanchions and damaged small and large vessels alike.

> *I remembered when I came in the next morning and saw all the boats up on the dock. It became pretty clear. We had thirty boats in the water. Two forty-footers and two twenty-footers ended up floating over the dock and ended up on the bulkhead. The only thing that kept them where they were was because they backed up against the machine shop in our building, otherwise they would have gone across the street.*
>
> *The first thing we had to do was to clear a path. You could not walk through any building or any spot. There was debris everywhere. We had to spend a couple of days clearing paths to walk. Then it snowed. Then we made arrangements for a crane. At the same time there was the gas crisis—people just showing up with no boat here just wanting to climb on a boat and take gasoline out of it. We had to lock down the yard. A lot of my friends in Freeport had to sleep in their trucks to protect their boats. That was another whole job on top of securing the boats and everything else. We went from being six feet under water to within days having equipment and trucks running.*
>
> *In the winter, we were trying to figure out how to fix everyone and get them out boating again. One thing we didn't do was to set the anchor off in the canal and tighten it up, so as the tide came up it would pull the*

"We went from being six feet under water to within days having equipment and trucks running." *Courtesy of Dan Schmidt.*

> *boat away from the dock. That would have proved to help us out—but we missed that on this storm. But having the buildings saved us.*
>
> *This particular storm showed that it's a really good place for a boat yard. Only a few other places have buildings. It's nice to have, but if it doesn't pay for itself—you can't maintain it. That's the problem. How much economic damage was done: property and time? Time is measurable but irreplaceable. You have to look at it as a lesson learned. The value that came out of that was how we all pulled together to get where we are today. Here's a perfect example—Wally—it was his first full year of being in charge of hauling all the boats. He said, "Wow I used skills I haven't used in twenty years." For me it was eye-opening to see someone young in the business to see that. Made me think of when I was a kid with Oliver Davison, when he moved boats—which if you told somebody—you would say "no way." We didn't have the equipment we have today.*

Despite the success Davison's had in recovering, in 2015 Schmidt sold the boat yard, a fate common in the boat yard industry on Long Island. The losses Schmidt sustained after Superstorm Sandy were astronomical, since most boat yards cannot afford flood insurance. Today there are condominiums on the property.

16

TOOMEY BOATYARD AND PEARL GREY MARINE

Amityville

Bud Toomey, the founder of the Toomey Boatyard, grew up with salt water in his veins.

> *My father from the time I was two years old enjoyed boating. My father came out to Amityville before I was born as a summer resident. In the early 1930s, he bought a house on Franklin Street, in Amityville. And that's where I grew up. He always loved boats and loved fishing. It rubbed off on me. When I was six years old, he got me a rowboat. I used to row around in the canals. That started me into boating.*

One of Bud's mentors was Johnny Becker, who was a boat builder in Amityville. As Bud recalled,

> *I used to go there in the wintertime when I wasn't working—because the fishing station would be closed down. I would go up there and help them when he was building boats. He would build them anywhere from twenty-six to thirty-five feet. I learned a lot from him. He created a lot of interest in me in learning how to do some boat work—not a craftsman by any means—but I did learn a lot from him. I would go up there and help him when he was building boats.*

Bud learned how to steam wood, how to make lapstrake planks, but he preferred running the bait station and the rowboat business.

Mary Toomey (Bud's sister), Phil (customer) and Buddy Toomey at the fishing station, 1955. *Courtesy of the Toomey family.*

In 1954, the Toomeys purchased a rundown fishing station they transformed into a rowboat rental and fishing shop for recreational fishermen. It was a welcome change of pace from working in New York City's financial district. In the 1960s, they began building their own boats. "They were built out of plywood, sixteen feet long and about five feet wide. They had high sides on them and were pretty nice boats," recalled Bud. "Most of my customers all came from the city—New York and Brooklyn. The Italians used to come out to go crabbing and clamming and they were characters—they made you laugh. This was when we used to tow boats out—because back then they didn't have much money—couldn't afford to buy a motor. So we used to tow them out to the bay." Theodora Toomey, known as Teddy, would sand boat bottoms and also do bottom painting alongside the yard workers. As a young girl, she considered herself a "tomboy" and was happy to work on boats.

The Toomeys had many customers, including some who were not knowledgeable about water navigation and often encountered difficulties on the south shore where boats could easily run aground during outgoing or low tides. Bud remembered one customer in particular.

One guy came in and said he knew how to run a boat. Lenny asked, "Have you ever driven a boat?" And he said yes, "I know all about it." He said, "You want me to show you a little bit? He said, "No. I know all about it." He gets out and goes down the canal backward. With the stern side and motor in reverse. Lenny had to yell, "Wait! Wait! In America we turn around and go bow first." And he was so insistent that he knew everything about boats and didn't need any instruction. After those lessons if anyone ever said that to me, I automatically got in the boat and showed them how to do it.

The yard provided many recreational fishermen with supplies so that they could rent them a small fishing boat. This included crab nets; fishing poles; and squid, killies and shiners for bait. They caught their own bait using traps they built from scratch. Most of their customers had their own fishing poles and lures. The Toomeys also sold hooks and sinkers. "We tried to have an array of stuff for them."

When their sons Michael and John were born, Bud and Teddy raised them to work and play on the water. As Bud recalled in 2011,

When Michael was very young, we gave him a garvey. When he was ten, eleven years old—he could run a thirty-footer. If we were going out for the weekend, he would take it from Purdy Lane and run it over to the boat yard and have it gassed up for us to be ready to go. The rule was you never went on a boat by yourself. Mike took his friend around with him. Then they left together, went home and after I got home, Michael said, "Mom I had a little problem with the boat." When he was tying it up, he stepped on the hatch which wasn't put on right and almost fell in the boat. He didn't have his friend with him. He never told me he dropped his friend off on the way home. We always told him that's why the rule is you're never on a boat by yourself.

During his teenage years, Michael learned how to fix engines, haul boats out of the water and other essential jobs at the yard. His parents shared this story with us:

One time, Bud had to have an engine out in a friend's boat. Mike was only thirteen. We were in Florida. Our friend calls up, "Bud you were supposed to put this engine in my boat." "Well, I'm in Florida. If you're in a rush, we'll have Michael do it." He's like, "I'm not going to have this thirteen-

Right: Teddy Toomey caulking and sanding John Wiswald's boat. *Courtesy of the Toomey family.*

Below: "In the thirty years running the Tiki Bar, we didn't have the cops there more than three times," remarked Teddy. *Photo by Nancy Solomon, 2011.*

> *year-old lower an engine into my boat." Then Bud was like, "You're going to have to wait till I come back from Florida." So he didn't want to wait and gave Michael a chance to do it. Michael did it so perfectly that he called Bud and told him, "I don't want you to touch my boat anymore. I only want Michael to do it." He just had that natural knack running engines and running boats.*

Today, the yard focuses on boat and mechanical repairs. In 1966, a small fire destroyed one of their buildings. Rather than replace the structure, the family decided to build a modest outdoor bar, which survives today. The cost of insurance put the rental boats out of business. "People came out, built homes, had dock space right in their backyards or went to the boat yards near their homes and asked if they can dock their boats there."

Many boat yards have suffered when storms and hurricanes strike. In order to protect the yard, they would tie down anything that could move. During Hurricane Gloria in 1985, the water did not enter their buildings but caused significant damage to their machinery, such as the boat lifts and forklifts. In 1991, "the perfect storm" came to Long Island gradually. As Michael recalled, "The preparation part was hard. You had to get your stuff out of the water in three days—and had to get everyone else's boats out too. When the storm was gone, everyone wanted fifty boats back in the water in the same day."

In April 2013, I was able to interview Michael and John about their experiences during Superstorm Sandy. They recalled,

> *Some of the first things done, the first couple of days was just monitoring and see what it looks like it might be. But then as it started getting a little closer. It wasn't supposed to come this time of year, but the European model predicted it was to hit New Jersey or New York Harbor. We started moving items upstairs little by little, kind of sitting back, wondering if we should take this seriously. We kept thinking it's late October—we're not supposed to be worrying about hurricanes now. The Atlantic is cool—that should be a plus on our side. Everything shouldn't be what it turned out to be.*

Like other yard owners, they put their boats on blocks and took as many boats as possible out of the water into their buildings, just days before the storm struck. While many expected water levels to rise, most thought it would only be three and a half to four feet. Instead, the storm surge was over ten feet. Most boats fell off their stands, inside and outside. Michael

The Toomey yard post Superstorm Sandy. *Photo by Nancy Solomon, 2013.*

and John lived next door to the yard, so they saw the boats being dislodged and crashing into each other. Other boats floated down the street. The only boats that stayed in place were those that remained in the canal.

Their friend Pete Hammond recalled, "We prepared by having a bunch of lines ready to try and catch the boats before they got away. That was an effort in futility—too much water to deal with. We let them float and decided to pick them up tomorrow."

Repair skills were sorely needed after Superstorm Sandy, as Michael recalled in 2013, shortly after the storm. "Out of the fifty boats—we had a couple of boats sitting on top of poles, and five got totaled. Now it's April—it will take us until August to sort through everything. A lot of the boats are a mess." John and Mike said, "We can deal with another ten Irenes but not another Sandy."

17

PAUL KETCHAM

Boat Builder and Restorer
Amityville

Paul Ketcham Jr. was born in Amityville in 1935 in his father's boat shop and house on New Point Place in Amityville. As a young boy, Paul helped remove sand from the creek so that boats could get onto the marine railway tracks into his grandfather's house. During the Depression, Paul's family settled in Florida, where his father worked in the Daytona Boat Works. In 1944, following the death of his grandfather, Paul's family returned to Amityville.

Growing up in Amityville, Paul helped his father with the maintenance and construction of various wooden boats; primarily skiffs, garveys and powerboats. Paul feels that boat builders are the opposite of carpenters because "everything they do is crooked while everything a carpenter does is straightened. With a wooden boat, when you get the form you still have to put it together. But a lot of people like the wooden boats because they're solider; the stuff we build around here [would] just run through a fiberglass boat."

Paul once said, "A boat builder has to have good eyes to see and share everything. If a boat builder doesn't have good eyes, they can screw up." Paul's earliest memory of building boats is coming home and helping his father decking down or some other stuff. As he recalled in 2011, "When my father first started working it was all hand tools. Bracing bits, no electric. Warren Purdy had one electric drill, and that was it. And everything else was all hand." Paul began working for his father in 1958, learning the principles and practice of traditional wooden boat building along the way. "When we

Paul Ketcham and his father, Paul, circa 1980. *Photo by Oliver Darling.*

were building the skiffs, it was about a hundred degrees in here. We could hardly see across the room. I would say about seventy skiffs were built from that steam box. I did most of it with the hand tools. My father was an expert on sharpening hand saws."

Many traditional boat builders began their projects by building a wooden model, a tradition that continues today. "A lot of times, the old timers would make a half model and then go from there. You would bend a piece of wood around the right thickness, and if it bends around the model, then you know it bends around the boat." During the time Paul worked for his father, he learned many of these skills and was fortunate to inherit his father's tools. Upon his father's retirement, Paul purchased the business in 1991. "About twenty years ago I bought it from my father: he didn't give it to me, I had to buy it. I got a lot of his old tools, all his old frames, and I was pretty well set."

Paul used routers, jigsaws and grinders, along with a modern electric planer that he purchased for $900 in 2000 for times when working with two different types of wood on repair jobs. The jigsaw was especially helpful to him "because, when making boats, you have to do things like get inside, quick turns, and stuff like that." Paul also used a bandsaw to cut out wood pieces for making planks.

The Ketchams, circa 1980. *Photo by Oliver Darling.*

A lot of the patterns Paul used for the boats came from his father. Paul and his father also designed a boat together. When making the patterns, he and his father drew them out. They would bend a piece of wood around the thickness. Their strategy was that if it bends around the middle then the boat can be built. Paul reflected that "for many boat builders, if they get an idea in their head and they want to build the boat, then they do it especially if they have the wood and time!" Paul finds it to be plain old fun. He also finds it to be a lot of fun to build your own boat instead of taking a plan and going from there. "The console for a twelve-foot Boston Whaler came in all falling apart. I scraped it down and got it back to its nice-looking wood."

Paul's boat building work gradually shifted toward boat maintenance "when all the old wooden boats came in here to be repaired, around thirty years ago" in the early 1980s. This shift reflected the increasing popularity of fiberglass boats and changes in the price, quality and availability of longleaf yellow pine, plywood, cypress, teak and mahogany. Paul recognizes the boats he has built because they have a shear to them. "If you have fiberglass boats that look like they are going to die, then you can put a shear on them and put a little bit of flair on them then they look halfway decent. Some of my clients just want room, and they don't care about how it looks. However, for many people, when a boat doesn't look good to them, they don't want to work on the boat."

Paul Ketcham and customer Chris Lister. *Photo by Oliver Darling.*

In 2001, Paul began using Spanish cedar for "patching up boats….They have a hell of a smell and an awful taste. But it bends good, it works good, and is a nice-looking wood; it almost looks like mahogany." Like other builders, Paul preserved his and his father's patterns, which can be used for building new wooden boats. Until he retired, he would go to Condon's lumberyard in White Plains, along with other boat builders featured in this book. He regularly used his steam box, located in his shop, to bend wood. Typical steam boxes are twenty-five to thirty feet long. It was last used in 2009 to build a garvey. Paul estimates that he built forty garveys in his lifetime. He has also built pleasure boats of various sizes, from twenty to forty feet, that are used on the south shore. However, he recognizes that most of his business has centered on repairing, rather than building boats. "There's not too many people around who can repair wooden boats because they don't know what it's all about."

When Superstorm Sandy approached Long Island, Paul kept his boats in the canal behind the yard, tying them to poles so that they would rise and fall with the tide. The two boats he had in the shop remained there. "If it floats off the blocking and lands on something—it will put a hole in it. If it's tied against something in the creek—it just goes up and down. A dock can destroy them. Tie them off the dock and keep them on the water" is Paul's advice to boat owners. Unfortunately, the tools suffered greatly. To make

Paul Ketcham and one of his garveys with Pete Petrucci. *Courtesy of the Ketcham family.*

The Ketcham boat yard. *Photo by Nancy Solomon, 2011.*

them usable again, Ketcham soaked them from two to twenty-four hours in WD-40 and then put them in fresh water. "If I had to work steady to make a living—I would be in big trouble."

When I asked Paul had the shop suffered from other storms or hurricanes, he said no, because "I have a sump pump so it can keep the water down three or four inches down on floor. I kept the pumps going." Ironically, the electricity failed, and so did the pumps, which was a blessing in disguise. The doors flew open and let some of the water out. Otherwise, the whole shop would have filled up with water and collapsed. Paul's dock and railway escaped serious damage from Sandy. "The dock is fine, that's plastic. The boardwalk I nailed down with ten to sixteen penny spikes, so that all stayed there. My father always taught me to do it a little overkill, but it pays."

After Hurricane Sandy and sustaining a knee injury, Paul retired and sold the Ketcham boatyard. "There are not enough wooden boats to hire somebody to do work, and there is too much involved to hire somebody. So if I can't do it that's it."

18

YACHT SERVICE

Amityville

I first learned about Amityville's nautical heritage from a local resident and historic preservationist, attorney Richard Handler. He had restored a catboat built in the nineteenth century and offered to take me around its harbor. Surrounding the small creek islands were a variety of boat yards with remnants of marine railways from years past. One of the yards was Yacht Service, owned by Steve Brice. According to Brice, the Amityville Creek islands were formed when barges dredged the east side. Steve has fond memories of growing up on Amityville Creek. "I grew up on this street. My dad had the powerboat, and I had the little runabout boat and a little sailboat, so boating is a bit in my blood. Ever since I bought this place, I have been extremely happy." Steve first got his start in the business while working for Jim's Boatyard during the summer of 1962 and 1963.

In 1973, Steve Brice purchased Yacht Service, a boat yard that was situated on two Ocean Avenue properties in Amityville, from Bob Schwarzler. Brice was the third owner of the site. "On the building that used to be here there was a sign with the ferry schedule on it. People used to get on at the Coles Avenue dock which was only a hundred feet from here. The ferry boats *Atlantic*, *Colombia* and *Adele* used to operate here around 1905."

The northern property at 144 Ocean Avenue was formerly known as Jim's Boatyard, where Brice worked in the 1960s. The southern property on 152 Ocean Avenue dates to the early twentieth century as the Wicks Boatyard, later known as the Ocean Avenue Boatyard. The Wicks yard was well known

Ferry boats depart Amityville, circa 1906. *Courtesy of Amityville Historical Society.*

for powerboats and the *Commodore*, a seventy-foot schooner built in 1912 for John Vanderveer of West Islip. Other yards built traditional skiffs for clammers and baymen in the area. In 1990, Steve bought a third property, doubling the size of Yacht Service, which continues to focus on the repair and storage of fiberglass boats.

Steve Brice, the owner, estimates that the last boat built in the yard was in the 1960s. When Steve first acquired Yacht Service, it sold O'Days, S2 and Hunter sailboats. "In the late 1980s when we stopped selling sailboats, when the store business started to falter and when the wholesale business started to die off, we went more into the service end."

In 1986, he removed the small railway on the property and bought a ten-ton travel lift. Steve recalled the changing demands of a service yard: "I kept the big railway for the big wooden powerboats to haul them out. It was good money. But slowly they disappeared, and they weren't being replaced. In 2003, I only had four big powerboats left, so I closed the big railway and bought a thirty-ton travel lift."

In 2008, Steve sold the business to his son Todd, who continues to operate the yard. As Steve recalled in 2011, "We were 85 percent sailboats. My son has gone a little more into the powerboats and now we are working on around 60 percent powerboats. When I sold the business to my son, I said I

The doors on the building cover the location of a former railway. *Photo by Nancy Solomon, 2008.*

wanted to work for three years; this is now the fifth year. As long as my body holds out fine, I'll still do it."

"The most fun part of running the yard is you have absolutely no idea what is going to occur five minutes from now let alone tomorrow. It is diversified; no day is the same for all the years I've been in business." At the same time, there are challenges, including receiving payment for the work they do: "People will come down on Sundays and take their boat. You don't go to a grocery store and not pay for the groceries. The culture in the boating business is we'll pay when we get around to it. We have to go chasing after it. We've always gotten paid, but people figure, we're their bank. People will come at night. It's irritating. But with very few exceptions people always pay."

Like other yards, there is always a shortage of qualified people who can work on boats. Brice brings in mechanics who work on specific projects at a variety of yards in the area. As he recalled,

The most important thing I learned way back is that your success is dependent on you, not your boss. I'm here because I did some all-nighters and I worked hard. Back in the beginning I would finish at 11:00 p.m./12:00 a.m. Then I came inside to do all the wholesale business and make orders to manufacturers. I also made phone calls to customers at night about buying boats. I think the future of the yard looks quite good. My son has done very well in soliciting new customers, and he has brought in some new thoughts.

19

DEGARMO BOATYARD

Babylon
Ted DeGarmo, Former Manager and Owner

I first met Ted DeGarmo at the Tobay Boat Show, organized by the New York Marine Trades Organization. Ted sat on the board of the nonprofit, which advocates on behalf of marine-oriented businesses. Ted DeGarmo was the owner and manager of DeGarmo's Boatyard in Babylon, established in 1910 by Captain Theodore Jay Watts, the captain of a sailing ship for the DeGarmo family. According to Ted,

> *The tradition in those days was for the foreman to invite the captain to stay at his house while the ship was out of the water. At the house, Theodore met the shipyard foreman's daughter and got married to her. He didn't want to go back to sea. Shipyard foremen were powerful people in those days, and he got a job as a policeman—he skipped the entry-level positions and went straight to detective. Theodore and his wife had four daughters when his house burned down. They came out to Babylon to stay at his former boss's home, Clarence DeGarmo, in Babylon. He liked it so much he bought property on Fire Island, where he built a small home, and bought another home in Bay Shore. Very quickly after that he started a boat yard. By 1911, he was in business.*
>
> *The people who first worked for him at the boat yard were his four daughters. He had no sons. During the war we had around three hundred employees.*

Theodore Watts founded the boatyard in 1910. *Courtesy of Ted DeGarmo.*

The earliest boats constructed at the yard were "mostly small boats with trunk cabins. They used them to go to Brooklyn—early in the morning—to get ice. They would be back by 7:00 or 8:00 p.m. They would also bring back kerosene because most lamps in those days were kerosene."

Over time, the yard grew as more people moved to Babylon.

> *By World War II, there were ninety people working there. We had different shops: machine shops—made propeller shafts, reconditioned propellers, made rudders—most of the people in the machine shop and boat repairs were Ukrainians. We also had woodworking shops—mostly Norwegians worked there. There was a large Ukrainian community in West Islip, and they were good workers. At that time, people were very proud so we needed to have lockers rooms so that they could change into and from street clothes. They had to have showers available for them at night—put street clothes back on and go home. It was also tradition—every one of them did it—for their wives to be there at noon on Friday for the paycheck.*

Like other boat yards, the DeGarmos benefitted from the Navy contracts with Grumman.

Ted DeGarmo. "The biggest change in the industry was probably when we went from wood to fiberglass." *Photo by Nancy Solomon, 2012.*

> *A lot of yards got significant work because of the military. During World War II, we were very fortunate—my father, Mr. Grumman and another principal at Grumman, Edward Pore, lived in Bay Shore, and was wealthy and had nice boats. We always took care of his boats. When the war began, the Navy offered machines at a lease rate of one dollar. We made parts for various Grumman aircraft during World War II but did not work on Navy boats because the bay was too shallow. Before the war the yard built mostly carvel planked boats; after the war lapstrake skiffs became more common.*

Most of the DeGarmo boat yard customers were from New York City, says Ted.

Ted estimates that four to five boats would have been built in the winter season during the boat yard's heyday, as "it was extremely labor-intensive work." During the spring and summer seasons, the yard was busy with maintenance demands. Material for the boats "always came from Brooklyn; Black and Yates was the big distributor of mahogany." The DeGarmo family was also a dealer for Owens, Chris-Craft and several smaller boat companies, selling "close to three hundred new boats a year." At its height,

Remnants of the circa 1973 office building after Superstorm Sandy. *Courtesy of Ted DeGarmo.*

the yard consisted of a marine supply store, a boat show room, a machine shop, a building shop, the boat yard and a restoration shop.

Before it closed in 2014, the yard had "downsized considerably because of the economy." In 2013, Ted estimated that they worked on "200 to 250 boats a year." Superstorm Sandy caused significant damage to the yard. The office building built in 1973 was destroyed. "Everything was either in the bay or in a big pile of junk. Never saw anything like it in my life. There was a lot that we lost in that building, including the history of the boat yard. We lost all of our photographs, our old canvas shop, sewing machines, inventory, parts and our entire stock of oil filters." As Ted recalled shortly after the storm, "There is no preventing a catastrophe like Sandy; it would be like preventing tornados in the Midwest. You can't do it: all you can do is try not to do anything foolish, so you don't get yourself killed. If you have a hurricane, the coastline is not the place to be; it is as simple as that." Ted was concerned for the future of the industry, as "the basis of our entire business here is family boating, and families are being hit hard by property taxes and expenses."

20

CHARLIE BALSAMO

South Bay Boat Repair
Patchogue

In 1994, the South Shore Estuary Reserve was formed to help maintain local waterfront traditions, support local maritime businesses and preserve the Great South Bay's ecological resources. As one of the early advocates for the plan, I met several people from Patchogue, who urged me to visit Charlie Balsamo at the South Bay Boat Repair yard, located on River Road in Patchogue, just up the river from Weeks Boat Yard. They told me he would be open to sharing his stories of the historic yard and of his business, which had changed profoundly over the years. Through the years, we've worked together, despite the challenges Charlie has faced, which you will read about. Fortunately, he has been able to continue working, despite his advancing years.

Charlie Balsamo, the yard's manager, was working on several projects when I first met him at the yard, tucked along the Patchogue River, once home to many boat yards. Balsamo was dedicated to the vanishing art of restoring and maintaining historic wooden craft. Balsamo, who started working at the yard in 1959, was born in Gibraltar. Charlie became a carpenter's apprentice when he was twelve years old. "I worked on the docks fixing boats" and later for the British government. When Balsamo arrived in the United States in 1959, "there were between the painters, mechanics and carpenters about twenty-six people working on the boats. They had three people in the office, five to six people in the stockroom, and the owner Eddie Wayne worked too."

Right: Charles Balsamo. *Photo by Nancy Solomon, 2006.*

Below: South Bay Boat Repair is best known for its work on wooden vessels like the *Lauren Kristy*, a tour boat. *Photo by Nancy Solomon, 2006.*

South Bay Boat Repair was founded as the Bishop Boat yard in about 1892 by George Bishop, a ship's carpenter. Bishop built fishing boats for John Doxsee's Deep Sea Fish Company in Islip, scows and oyster steamers for the Westerbeke Brothers oyster company and "dredging steamers" for the Vanderborgh oyster company of West Sayville. During Prohibition, the yard was a commonly used site for shipping illegal liquor, as were other boat yards on Long Island.

The boat yard once boasted several historic structures, including a well-preserved marine railway. "The rails were used for hauling larger boats—over one hundred foot—pleasure and fishing boats, freight boats, all kinds of work boats, oyster boats." A historic barn made from recycled timbers from neighboring structures in the 1920s survived the 1938 hurricane, which caused significant damage in the waterfront areas of town. During Charlie's tenure at the yard, approximately seventy-five boats were built and repaired, including commercial fishing boats, Coast Guard vessels and ferry boats. Like other yards, demand decreased in the 1980s as fiberglass replaced wooden boats. "I remember when they built three boats at a time. The party boats would be stacked in the creek, waiting to be hauled out, one alongside the other, waiting their turn."

South Bay Boat Repair was best known for its work on large-scale wooden vessels like the *Lauren Kristy*, a tour boat owned by Mike Eagan, based in Bay Shore. "People got rid of wooden boats because marinas are scared they are going to sink. I like wooden boats. It costs more money than a fiberglass boat because it takes longer to make. They're made piece by piece. Every day is a different thing—you learn as you go." According to patrons, "Charlie could always do whatever you needed done. Charlie is the best in the business. He always took time out to explain things." As Charlie explained, "The problem with a lot of people is they don't want to buy wooden boats and don't want to spend any money on it. Ninety percent of the marinas do not want to take wooden boats. Most of the wooden boats they build now are in Maine, Virginia and Maryland. But around here not too many people are building them anymore." One of Charlie's customers, Joe Brown, commented that "he has an unlimited knowledge of shipbuilding and boat building."

South Bay was just one of several boat yards along the Patchogue River, including the legendary Gil Smith boat yard, where catboats dominated. Today the last survivors are South Bay and Weeks Boat Yard. Sadly, the owner of South Bay Boat Repair removed the historic marine railway in 2009 to make room for a marina, despite calls for its preservation. A large historic "barn" was also removed. Balsamo continues to restore majestic

In 2008, the marine railway was removed, and in 2009 the owner demolished the historic "barn" over Balsamo's objections. *Photo by Nancy Solomon, 2007.*

wooden craft, including a historic cruiser from the early twentieth century. A regular group of boat owners gathers each morning to share their challenges of maintaining their boats and remember how Patchogue used to be, full of different types of boats, including ferries and party boats that took people fishing or transporting them to Fire Island. They are dedicated to preserving this historic yard and supporting Charlie.

21

FRANK M. WEEKS YACHT YARD

Patchogue

In 2004, Long Island Traditions was asked to conduct a maritime cultural resource survey for the South Shore Estuary Reserve Council, under the guidance of New York's Department of State. One of the communities documented was the Village of Patchogue, where we found several examples of working waterfront businesses, including the Weeks Yacht Yard. Graduate school intern Jayme Breschard Thomann of Cornell University conducted an intensive survey, along with Long Island Traditions' staff folklorist Chris Muia. We interviewed both Brian Weeks, now deceased, and his brother Kevin Weeks, who currently runs the yard. The yard is perhaps one of the best-preserved boat yards on Long Island and continues to carry on the legacy of generations of boat builders. For those interested in seeing the yard, we suggest you go to Trunzo Park on the Patchogue River across from the boat yard.

Frank M. Weeks was born into a family on River Avenue in Patchogue that has made its home there since the early 1700s. Born in 1883, he was the son of Lafayette Weeks, a merchant who served as an officer in the Union army. During the Battle of Gettysburg, his father was wounded and captured by the Confederates. Today, his descendants, Weeks family members, operate one of the oldest family-run boat yards in the United States.

As a young boy, Frank Weeks was fascinated by boats and boating. After finishing school, he worked full time for Martinus Smith, who owned and operated a shipyard on some of the land that is today Weeks Yacht Yard. After his apprenticeship with Smith, Weeks became a master carpenter and

Above: *Photo by Jayme Breschard Thomann, 2004.*

Opposite, top: *Photo by Jayme Breschard Thomann, 2004.*

Opposite, bottom: The Machine Shop was sighted to prevent flooding after the 1938 hurricane. *Photo by Jayme Breschard Thomann, 2004.*

shipwright. In 1898, he built and sold his first boat—a small cat sailboat named *Onion*. It is said that he paid for the building supplies for the boat by selling onions he grew behind his house.

Weeks purchased the land for the boat yard in small increments. He bought some land from Sophie K. Smith Petty, and in the 1920s, he bought more land from David B. Bannerman, a customer of his. As Kevin Weeks recalled, "My grandfather built a number of buildings I want to say between the years 1915 and 1923." By 1928, he had purchased all of the present property, approximately five acres. As compared to today, the physical features of the land were quite different. Brian Weeks recalled that "there were railroad tracks that led down into the river for launching the boats. There was no bulk heading, only a small peninsula of wetlands. Boat owners moored their boats out in the river on stakes."

FRANK M. WEEKS YACHT YARD

LYONS

Like most boat yard owners, "They followed the tradition that whenever they needed to do something around the yard, they did it themselves," according to Brian Weeks. "For example, his grandfather built the shops himself. He bought lumber from Bailey's—mahogany, oak and teak." Today they buy most of their wood from Condon's Lumberyard in White Plains.

Frank Weeks worked on a variety of vessels, including barges, ferries and commercial fishing boats. Kevin Weeks said that his grandfather constructed "shoal draft, the barges that were used to ship lumber, coal and other supplies from New York City out to Long Island. My grandfather, I believe, continued doing that sort of building when he started his own business."

The oldest buildings in the yard have dirt floors for good reasons. As Brian Weeks recalled, "Our dirt floor barns are actually very good for the wooden boats. They tend to stay damp and moist throughout the winter and the early spring. And they don't dry out in there." Weeks built and designed many types of boats in his lifetime. In his youth, perhaps the most famous vessel he worked on was the *Grace E. Bailey*, a schooner built before the turn of the century that still exists today in Camden, Maine. This boat was actually built in front of the oldest building in the yard and perhaps in Patchogue. He also built boats designed by John Alden and other renowned designers.

As he gained experience, Frank Weeks built different lines of sailboats and powerboats. For example, he built hundreds of Fire Island one-design nineteen-foot sailboats, which sold for approximately $250. He was also known for building local designs such as the Narrasketucks and South Bay Scooters. He may have also built rumrunning boats during Prohibition in the 1930s. Unfortunately, many of the Weeks Boat designs and half models he used in making a boat were destroyed by fires at the boat yard in the 1940s through 1950. However, Weeks's original tools and machinery are still used in the yard today. He employed a small staff to help him with his work. The boat yard had begun building its reputation for quality work and service.

In addition to his boat building skills, Weeks built and maintained many of the buildings/sheds for the yard. He bought many of his materials from Bailey's Lumber Yard in Patchogue. One exception was the main building, which underwent extensive renovations in 2004. Originally an officer's mess at Camp Upton, a World War I training camp, Weeks had it moved in two pieces to the boat yard and built a second floor for storage.

For recreation, Weeks was an expert yacht and sailboat racer. Weeks was named as a superior yachtsman by the *New York Times* sporting section at the time. He has passed down his love of racing to the next generations of his family. Frank Weeks died in 1966, having spent his final years in Florida. He saw the successful transition to the full-service marina and was a proud grandfather to four grandchildren: Jeffrey, Dale, Kevin and Brian.

Weeks Yacht Yard in the 1950s–1980s

Frank Weeks and his wife, Carrie, had three sons and one daughter from 1915 to 1930. The three brothers, Frank V. Weeks, Joseph and David, grew up around the water and the business. After serving in World War II, brothers Frank and Joe took over operations for this family business and were later joined by brother David, after he served in Korea. Their father retired in the late 1950s, and the sons took to modernizing the business as they saw fit.

As Kevin Weeks recalled in 2004, "Dave and Joe and Frank made the place more into a marina where we did boat repairs and some building." Brian and Kevin began working at the yard when they were very young. Brian built his first boat at age twelve. "My dad and I built a boat about ten feet long" based on plans from a Canadian company, modifying it for the shallow bay waters. The two brothers worked together, eventually taking over the yard when their father passed away in 1995.

There was a shift in the boat building industry in the 1970s when the boat yard owners moved more towards boat maintenance, while keeping their hand in boat building. During the 1960s, they designed and built approximately fifteen to twenty twenty-six-foot Weeks Sea Skiffs from wood materials. In 2004, approximately 75 percent of their work was restoring wooden boats, according to Brian. "People get sentimental about wooden boats."

It was also during this time that the brothers made some physical changes to the yard. Slowly, bulkheading was added to the yard, eliminating most of the wetland peninsulas. To meet the demands of being a marina, as well as a boat building yard, travel lifts were also purchased. Winter storage for boats was provided by designating sheds for that use. One building was equipped with railways to transfer the boats. Weeks employed approximately thirteen staff, but that could fluctuate given the economy. At one time when business was high, Brian Weeks remembered having twenty workers.

WEEKS YACHT YARD FROM THE 1980S TO THE PRESENT DAY

Today, the family-run boat yard continues its boat building traditions combined with being a full-service marina. It is run by Kevin Weeks and their staff of approximately eleven to sixteen people, both full- and part-time. As a marina, the yard can store over 120 boats of different sizes and has over sixty dock slips available for rentals. Although boat repair is the yard's main source of business, Weeks has been of the country's largest commercial producers of Detroit News (DN) iceboats since 1979. These are fourteen-foot winter boats, designed in 1938 through a contest in the Midwest and modernized by the Weeks boat yard.

The yard also builds fiberglass Force 5 sailboats. These are made from fiberglass using molds they designed and manufactured. The yard produces about four to five sailboats a year. Younger staff members learn more about the wooden boat building traditions taught by the older members of staff such as Chris Hale, a master boat builder and model maker.

During an interview in 2004, folklorist Chris Muia asked the late Brian Weeks what he remembered about this area in general growing up as a child and what changes he had seen in boat building over the years. Some of his reflections are as follows.

Brian remembered that the Patchogue River was much more industrial as compared to the recreational /residential feel it has now. He remembered seeing oil tanks/stacks and oil tankers going up and down the river. He remembered the Lace factory employing many people but wondered how much it was really polluting the river. He spoke about the weather patterns—hurricanes and other storms that passed through the area, especially Hurricane Gloria in 1985. Brian recalled the damage done by the storm to the buildings and the ingenuity employed by staff to shore up the buildings before the storm hit. He also witnessed the rise and fall of the clamming industry, at one time one of the largest waterfront industries on Long Island.

The yard has retained many of its original features. The marine railways remain, but they are no longer connected to the river. They are used to move boats within the yard. Brian was a committed historic preservationist alongside his brother Kevin. In 2004, Brian reflected, "All of these buildings are built on locust posts, but some are getting old and the buildings are settling. I'm seeing the sentimental value as well as the historical significance, especially as the rest of the river is changing almost on a monthly basis."

Kevin Weeks (*left*) and Brian Weeks. *Photo by Jayme Breschard Thomann, 2004.*

Kevin remarked that when Superstorm Sandy hit in 2012, they knew they would survive. "Someone marked the high-water mark at the machine shop after the 1938 hurricane. My dad and uncle used that in deciding in how high to raise the property here. Since 1938 until hurricane Irene in 2011, water never approached the bulkhead—ever—not once. In Irene and Sandy, it did. I never saw so much water here in my life, and I hope to never again."

22

CHRIS HALE, BOAT BUILDER AND MODEL MAKER

Medford

When I first visited the Weeks Yacht Yard in Patchogue in 2004, I saw Chris Hale working on restoring a historic wooden boat. Since that time, I have learned of Chris's many talents. Hale is one of the most accomplished boat half model makers and has devoted himself to making replicas of historic south shore wooden boats, including garveys, skiffs and catboats. He has worked at many boat yards on Long Island, including Coecles Harbor Marina on Shelter Island, at Hampton Shipyard in East Quogue and currently at Weeks Yacht Yard in Patchogue, where he has worked since the 1990s. He works on restoring traditional wooden boats ranging from skiffs and catboats to modern recreational fishing boats. At Weeks Yacht Yard, Hale is responsible for building fiberglass racing and pleasure boats. Hale is also one of the few boat builders who makes half models of traditional boats that once graced Great South Bay.

Hale follows a long line of traditional boat builders who make half models, a tradition that was carried on by Fred Scopinich of East Quogue when Fred worked at his family's Freeport Point Shipyard during the early to mid-twentieth century, Paul Ketcham and other traditional boat builders. Hale was born in Glen Cove Hospital and grew up in Massapequa. As Chris recalled,

> *My great-grandfather was a boat builder, and he had these three half models kicking around the beach house which I liked. We also used to go down to Sag Harbor a lot and look at the boats on the dock. Eventually,*

Chris Hale. *Photo by Nancy Solomon, 2013.*

> *we got a rowboat. But I always liked boats as a kid. I didn't know that you could get a job working on them. I thought they came from a magical place or something. I never gave it much thought until high school. And so that's my background with boating, having the beach house and seeing a lot of boats as a kid.*

When Hale graduated from high school, he pursued a career in boat building, an unusual choice in the late 1970s, by looking for a traditional boat building school.

> *Back in 1980, those were not expensive schools. They were trying to get people in them, and that's when I realized that I could learn how to do something and get a job, not just sweeping the floor, but actually cutting wood boards and then sweeping the floor. It was pretty good. I learned a lot at the trade school. I only went to one trade school. I went to the Landing Boat Shop which is in Arundel, Maine.*

Upon graduation, Chris worked at various boat yards on Long Island, including Sea Fair Yachts in Huntington, where he quickly rose through the ranks and became head of the wood shop, working on complex projects.

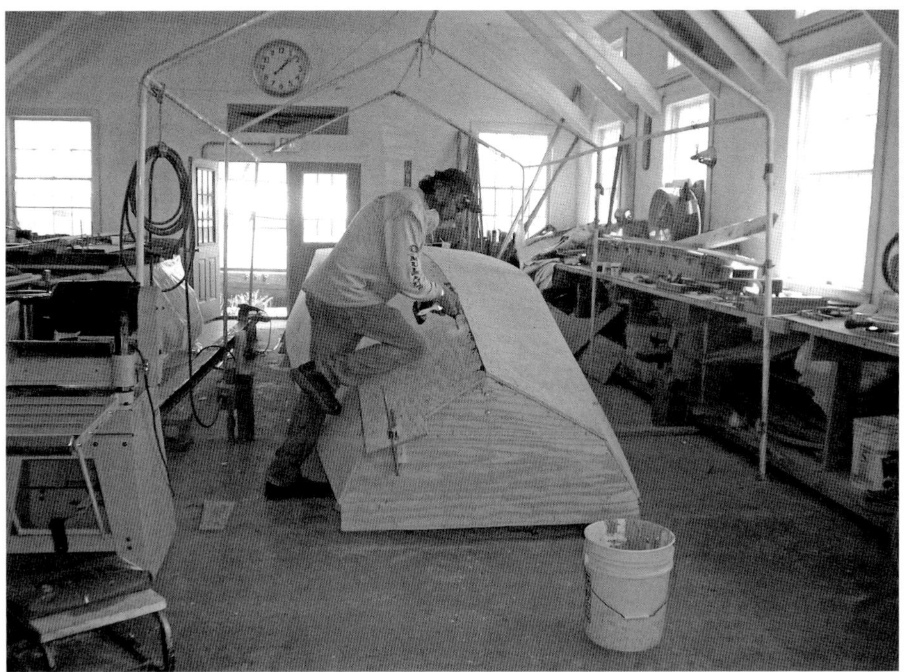

Chris Hale has constructed several garveys. This one was built in 2016. *Courtesy of Chris Hale.*

When Sea Fair closed in 1984, Hale attended Southampton College, earning a history degree. He also worked at the Hampton Shipyard run by the Scopinich family until 1990.

For several years, Chris worked independently on a variety of projects while also helping Anders Langendal and Al Grover. He traveled to North Carolina, where he worked at Gary Davis Boat Building, eventually returning to Long Island and working at Coecles Marine Harbor on some of Billy Joel's boats. In 1995, he met Brian Weeks and began working at the Weeks Boat Yard, where he remains today.

Hale began making models when he was attending the Landing School, a common requirement at boat building academies.

> *I was the youngest at the school. No one was making anything. I started constructing 3D models with scrap wood and cardboard, and that worked well. Then I started playing around with making half models. Once in a while I'd make a half model of a racing sailboat. I'd make one every few months and made them more and more. I've always liked the history of*

Garvey model by Chris Hale. *Photo by Nancy Solomon, 2011.*

> *sailboat racing. I like all boats, especially workboats—garveys, etc. I had a lot of access to local workboats. I started making folk art models of garveys and selling them. Locals would buy them.*

Chris makes several varieties of half models that include both recreational and commercial boats. Like other boat builders, Hale is self-taught, but he has learned many of the skills necessary for boat building and model making in a traditional format by emulating other more experienced builders.

Featured in a 2013 *Newsday* article, Hale told reporter Bill Bleyer, "My great-grandfather was a boat builder in Brooklyn in the late 1800s and early 1900s" and built half models as part of that business. He inherited three of his ancestor's workboat half models, which are now mounted on the wall of his living room. "I always thought they were kind of cool," Hale added.

Hale uses various types of wood depending on the model he is making. The most common types are mahogany, spruce and poplar. Using specialized tools, Hale makes garveys, models of sailing racing boats and other boats commonly found on Great South Bay. He starts with a single piece of wood and, using an architectural ruler, draws the profile on the wood. As Bleyer describes, "Once he has his assemblage of wood layers, he uses flat wood patterns to trace the side view on one side and the top-down view on the top, and make initial cuts in the shape of the hull on his electric band saw. Then, he'll spend a half-hour or more with an electric disk sander, then start doing finer work with the hand planes and finishing with hand sanding, repeating the cycle as necessary." Hale estimates that he has built over one hundred models and plans to continue for years to come.

A typical garvey half model is relatively simple to make since Hale has created patterns for the model. It will take him approximately an hour.

Left: Chris Hale participates in Long Island Traditions maritime school programs. *Photo by Nancy Solomon, 2018.*

Below: Elementary school students learn how to make models with Chris Hale. *Photo by Nancy Solomon, 2019.*

Other models are more complex; an America's Cup racing boat can take six hours. He uses a variety of tools, historic and contemporary, including vintage planes, along with power saws and sanders. Hale has built over six hundred half models. He estimates that he has restored over thirty wooden boats.

In addition to boat building and model making, Chris spent many years racing in competitive tournaments, including those sponsored by the Bellport Yacht Club. In early years, he used to race every weekend and would travel to other club's regattas. These days, he prefers working on models. "My favorite thing to do is to work on the models. Making models of all America's Cup boats. I want to build another boat, and I love restoring them. But my passion is making models."

23

STEIGER CRAFT

Alan Steiger, Founder and Owner
Bellport

When I started going to boat shows in the early 1990s, one of the things I kept hearing about was the Steiger Craft boat because of its ability to navigate the shallow bay waters of Long Island's south shore during low tide. Steiger Craft is almost a household name among boaters here, and for good reason. It is one of the largest boat builders on Long Island and has designed a time-tested vessel. When I first met Alan Steiger, he explained that "if you love your job, then you never have to go to work, which is true. I love what I do. Building boats and dealing with boats."

Steiger grew up clamming and fishing. As he recalled,

> *I was eleven years old when I started clamming. At twelve years old I got my first boat. My father and grandfather had boats, and both fished. My father worked for Suffolk County as a marine carpenter. He did a lot of stuff for the Sayville museum* [Long Island Maritime Museum]. *When he turned fifteen, Ron Overton, who worked at the Scopinich boat yard, built a sharpie for Alan. By age sixteen he was working on the bay harvesting clams. At age eighteen he built his first wooden boat, which he sold or traded for a motor or another boat. In the mid-1960s, it used to cost $200 to $300 to build a boat. $300 to $400 for a motor, then you would buy a clam rake, baskets and some other things. The license was $5. For $1,000 you were a clammer.*

Steiger Craft began as a clamming supply store founded by Alan Steiger in 1972.

> *When I started building boats I was a commercial fisherman: crabbing, clamming and gill netting…The reason I went into to this was because tongs break. Only one guy made them in Babylon named Klein. He didn't open til 3:00 p.m. You would wait in line with one hundred guys. You would wait three hours. Then he closed, and if you didn't get in, you didn't get them. So I started making them for myself. Then friends said "make me a set" and one thing led to another. I would go clamming in the morning. Then open at 11:00 a.m. and work til midnight. When I got hurt, I couldn't go to work—clamming. So I went to the shop thinking there would be no one there. There were people waiting since 9:00 a.m. So I stayed there and never went back to clamming.*

When he started the shop, he also built wooden boats on the side. Steiger's grandfather purchased the property in 1910. Alan Steiger always loved being on the water, whether he was fishing commercially or recreationally. His father was a marine carpenter, which is where he got his love for building and designing wooden boats. Although Steiger did not enjoy commercial fishing, "I always knew I wanted to do something with the water."

At first, Steiger built wood boats, similar to those built by Howard Pickerell, which were labor-intensive and time-consuming. In 1974, Steiger

Alan Steiger, the founder of Steiger Craft. *Photo by Nancy Solomon, 2012.*

began building fiberglass boats but did not shift to a full fiberglass frame until 1990, with the assistance of boat builder Eric Wright, owner of North End Marine in Maine.

> *When we first started to make fiberglass hulls, they had a wood stringer system, a wood floor and a wood deck that we put fiberglass over. Then we got away from the wood deck. As time went on, we eventually got rid of the wood stringers and wood floor. In the old days, we'd have a drawing of a boat, have blueprints. Then we would loft the hull, and that means we would take the blueprints, make like them life size. And build frames and loft the hull and then would skin the hull. And then we'd, after we did that, we would make the mold. And that's how we would make a boat.*

A few traditional elements remain, including wood transoms.

Steiger's main customers were local baymen due to the plentiful clam supply in the 1970s. Like Howard Pickerell, Steiger catered to the commercial fishermen and baymen. His boats were designed to go into shallow bay waters, where they could harvest clams, scallops, oysters and other shellfish. At one point, Steiger built three hundred boats a year—a

Molds for fiberglass boats. *Photo by Nancy Solomon, 2012.*

lot of them sixteen-footers. "Those are for the guys who went on little trailers, fishing." Over time, Steiger was able to fulfill orders placed by the National Park Service and the Coast Guard for local patrol boats used in search-and-rescue missions. The typical size was twenty-five to twenty-six feet long with a pilothouse because they wanted protection from the weather. The top speed was fifty miles per hour, but most owners cruise at thirty miles per hour.

In the late 1980s, Steiger noticed a demand for work boats to become pleasure boats. "They required some things the commercial guys didn't: rod holders, seating, a cooler in the console, a windshield and a handrail." Although Steiger Craft boats were originally designed for the shallow bay waters, in the mid-1990s Alan developed "Deep-V" bottom boats for deep-sea recreational fishing. As Steiger observed, "the fiberglass boat can break ice, was bigger, it has V-bottoms and it rowed better."

> *Fishing was real good. There were no restrictions. Pollution wasn't that bad. There was no Southwest Sewer District polluting everything. The oceans were cleaner. In the '70s and '80s there was an abundance of fish. You didn't have to go very far. The average guy would fill the boat with fish. Even sports guys would sell the fish because you couldn't eat all that fish, give them to friends and family.*

Steiger maintains that the advantage of a fiberglass boat continues to be its durability and lower maintenance costs. However, unlike building a wooden boat, where features such as the width of the hull can be modified, "with fiberglass you are restricted to the mold." In 1996, Steiger Craft offered a lifetime warranty, a practice that continues. "In the 1970s, we sold one hundred boats a year to them [baymen]. They were coming out of old wooden boats that were sinking. Our worst boat was a Cadillac to them. Those fiberglass boats are still in existence—they didn't fall apart—not biodegradable."

The larger V-Bottom boats are also suitable for ocean fishing, a major attraction for recreational fishermen on Long Island and elsewhere. As the population of commercial fishing declined, Steiger began building more boats tailored to sports fishermen. Today he sells that same one hundred boats each year, but they are sold to markets in New York, Connecticut, New Jersey, Virginia and Maine.

The boats have proven to be seaworthy for many generations. Occasionally, Alan received a letter from a customer thanking him for building such

One of the classic Steiger Craft boats. *Courtesy of Steiger Craft.*

durable vessels. "One guy told me that the boat flipped over and the boat didn't sink and so it saved his life."

Steiger's children have worked alongside him over the years. Today, Connor Steiger is the main person in charge. Thousands of people have worked for Steiger, some for several decades. As Alan approaches his later years, he reflects on his life history. "We designed boats to last forever. Because that's what I believe in."

24

HOWARD PICKERELL

Boat Builder and Bayman
Water Mill

For many years I had heard about Howard Pickerell from my colleague John Eilertsen, another folklorist and retired director of the Bridgehampton Historical Society. I got to know Howard slowly, since I was based in western Nassau County and he was nestled in Water Mill, near Southampton. Over time, we did programs together and gradually formed a bond that I value today.

Howard Pickerell is a traditional commercial boat builder and bayman born in Huntington. During his youth, he learned to harvest the abundant clams of Huntington from his father. As Howard recalled in 2007,

> *We live on an island here. Just about everybody back then had something to do with the water. I mean everybody, their part-time job was working on the water clamming. And they all did good. Back then we can do a bushel an hour. And a bushel was actually like six to seven hundred clams. I could find clams on the sidewalk. And most baymen can't find them. You know because they don't know how to work the bottom, edges and so forth. So if you don't show them where they are, they are never going to find them. I can find clams. If they are there, I'll get them.*

Howard began to build boats for sale in his teenage years, a tradition that he continues today. Howard built his first boat for sale when he was fourteen years old. As Howard recalled, "It was for a guy named Stubbings—an old bayman from Huntington. He used the boat for twenty-five years." Pickerell

Howard Pickerell. "I started out making garveys for my friends. I was paid $200 to $240. Now they are sold for $5,000." *Photo by Nancy Solomon, 2007.*

started out by making boats for friends, earning $200 to $240. One of Howard's major influences was his grandfather. "He was a carpenter—a house carpenter. That's probably where I picked up how to make boats—using tools. My father had a basic fourteen-foot rowboat that came from a New Haven sharpie." Howard was also a resourceful bayman able to make a healthy living. "We could harvest a bushel an hour, about six to seven hundred clams, at $8 a bushel. When I finished high school, I went on the bay full time."

As he became more committed to working as a bayman, Howard began looking at what made for a good workboat. "The garvey has a blunt bow also known as 'chicken breasted.' The sharpie is a pointed boat. The garvey is low sided, lays really low and carries a heavy load, which makes it very seaworthy." Like other earlier boats, oak was the preferred material and was available at local sawmills like Harned's Saw Mill in Commack. As it became scarcer, boat builders turned to red oak, which unfortunately rotted easily. He began using greenwood for the frame and marine plywood, which he still uses today, along with epoxy, as do other boat builders.

Howard had dozens of baymen who wanted to buy his boats. In 1979, he moved to Southampton, where he had strong connections to the East End baymen through his boat building business. His customers included the Lesters:

How can you not know the Lesters—Richie Lester, Stuart Lester, Stuart Vorpahl, Billy Schultz and Brad Loewen. I kind of blended in. For Brad I probably made him three boats. If you're from East Hampton, you had to have a sharpie. The only guy I converted over to garveys was Billy Schultz. He had fish traps. I put a well in the back so that he could tilt the motor up.

The main characteristics of a sharpie are a standard low bow and high sides.

Pickerell has built hundreds of garveys and sharpies. Although Pickerell prefers using a garvey, he knows that East End baymen prefer the sharpie because of their tradition. The designs have changed little over time; however, the materials have changed greatly. One of the reasons Pickerell's boats were in such high demand was the lucrative scallop business. "I had to change the design of the sharpie for scalloping—it has a straighter and higher side—the scallopers preferred it that way. It's more traditional. When your grandfather and his grandfather had that design, that's what you have to have." All during this time, Howard continued to work on the water, harvesting clams and scallops. Due to the decline of commercial fishing, there is no longer a need for Howard's boats. "I cater to the commercial guys, and commercial fishing is over. Now I build four or five boats a year." In 2003, Pickerell became one of the first east end baymen to grow and

A pair of thirty-two-foot lobster hulls "down easters" built for two Southampton fishermen in 1987–88. *Courtesy of Howard Pickerell.*

The *Lady Diane. Courtesy of Howard Pickerell.*

harvest oysters, due to the assistance of Cornell Cooperative Extension. He sells his oysters to white tablecloth restaurants.

Many of his boat customers are recreational, who prefer a traditional workboat design.

> *What I am doing with some of them, I'm taking my commercial hull and doing it real fancy, putting in center consoles and stuff like that. It's a pleasure to get in them, to know they're really seaworthy and strong boats. I finish them up real fancy and so forth. But it's still the same old boat, the same old design, you know. And some people rather than having something like a Clorox bottle, would like to have something traditional. If you live on Long Island, that's what you got to have.*

Pickerell also builds boats for town lifeguards and recreational fishermen in nearby communities. Howard's personal boat, the *Lady Diane*, is named after his wife. It is a thirty-two-foot craft with a split pilothouse "so that you can work the hauler. The hauler is under the top." The boat was built in 1985 as a model. Howard uses it for pleasure. When asked what the future holds for local baymen, he replied, "I don't think there will be any baymen left on the water. We live on an island, surrounded by pristine water, and we can't make a living on it."

BIBLIOGRAPHY

Balsamo, Charles. Interview by Nancy Solomon. January 14, 2006.

Bleyer, Bill. "LI Man Makes Art with Smaller Boats Models." *Newsday*, July 18, 2013.

Brice, Steven. Interview by Nancy Solomon. August 6, 2012.

Clarke, Steven. Interview by Nancy Solomon. April 24, 2012.

Costanzo, Donn. Interview by Nancy Solomon. March 14, 2012.

Costello, John. Interview by Nancy Solomon. May 16, 2012.

DeGarmo, Ted. Interviews by Nancy Solomon. August 6, 2012. January 30, 2013.

Grover, Al. Interviews by Nancy Solomon. May 5, 1987. May 13, 1987. November 6, 2014. November 19, 2020.

Hale, Chris. Interview by Nancy Solomon. April 21, 2021.

Harter, Robert, and Ron Harter. Interview by Nancy Solomon. July 11, 2011.

Heinz, Peter. Interview by Nancy Solomon. July 12, 2011.

Kenny, Charles. Interview by Nancy Solomon. October 26, 2011.

Ketcham, Paul. Interviews by Nancy Solomon. June 30, 2011. January 30, 2013.

Knutson, Dan. Interview by Anna Mule. July 7, 2011.

———. Interview by Nancy Solomon. October 16, 2012.

Langendal, Anders. Interview by Nancy Solomon. November 9, 2011.

Maresca, Everett. Interview by Nancy Solomon. January 3, 1990.

Maresca, Jerry. Interview by Nancy Solomon. January 11, 2016.

Needham, Peter. Interview by Nancy Solomon. November 9, 2011.

O'Reilly, James. Interview by Nancy Solomon. February 27, 2013.

Pickerell, Howard. Interview by Nancy Solomon. June 12, 2007.

Remsen, John. Interviews by Nancy Solomon. March 9, 2016. October 24, 1988. November 17, 2003.

Scanlan, Greta, and Charlotte Mullen. Interview by Nancy Solomon. September 28, 2012.

Schmidt, Dan. Interviews by Nancy Solomon. August 31, 2012. February 11, 2013.

Scopinich, Fred. Interview by Nancy Solomon. November 21, 1988.

Short, David. Interview by Nancy Solomon. January 5, 2012.

Steiger, Alan. Interview by Nancy Solomon. July 26, 2012.

Toomey, John, and Michael Toomey. Interviews by Nancy Solomon. September 22, 2011. April 23, 2013.

Toomey, John, Michael Toomey, Bud Toomey and Theodora Toomey. Interview by Nancy Solomon. October 24, 2011.

Waldo, David. Interview by Nancy Solomon. December 22, 2011.

Weeks, Brian. Interview by Chris Muia. August 4, 2004.

Weeks, Kevin. Interview by Nancy Solomon. March 6, 2013.

ABOUT THE AUTHOR

Nancy Solomon lived in Mamaroneck as a teenager across from Nichol's boatyard. After the school day ended, she rushed to the yard, where she learned firsthand how commercial lobstermen made their living, a challenging occupation. She also volunteered on the sloop *Clearwater*. While attending college and graduate school at George Washington University, Solomon focused on occupational cultural traditions of farmers and coal miners, and vernacular architecture. She received her master's degree in American Studies and Folklife Studies from George Washington University. Upon graduating, Solomon moved to Vermont, where she learned to supervise historic surveys of the state's communities. She lived there for two and a half years, all the time wishing she was closer to the ocean. When the Long Island Arts Council at Freeport advertised for a folklorist to document maritime cultural traditions in 1987, she packed her bags and has called Long Island home ever since.

Solomon is the executive director of Long Island Traditions, based in Port Washington. She is the author of *On the Bay: Bay Houses & Maritime Culture of Long Island*, *West Meadow Beach: A Portrait of a Long Island Beach Community* and *Traditional Architecture of Long Island: A Teacher Resource Guide*. She is a columnist for *Voices*, published by NY Folklore, and the Encyclopedia of American Studies Online. She is the curator of *Waterfront Heroes*, *In Harm's Way*, *Freeport Waters* along Freeport's Nautical Mile, co-curator of *From Shore to Shore: Boat Builders and Boatyards of Long Island and Westchester* and curator of *Sandy Shores: The Creation of Jones Beach*, a permanent outdoor exhibit along the Jones Beach bicycle path. Solomon was the primary advisor to filmmakers Barbara Weber and Greg Blank on their 2020 documentary *A World Within a World: Long Island's Bay Houses*. She also worked with Glenn Gebhard on his 1994 documentary *Baymen*. She was the historic preservation consultant to the Village of Great Neck Plaza and the maritime culture consultant to the South Shore Estuary Reserve. Solomon also works with the Village of Rockville Centre. Solomon has lectured extensively on historic preservation and documentation methods for Columbia University's Historic Preservation Program and area colleges.